TEACHING EFL ONLINE

AN E-MODERATOR'S REPORT

Further titles in this series

www.linguabooks.com

TEACHING EFL ONLINE

AN E-MODERATOR'S REPORT

Andrew R. Webster

Print edition: ISBN 978-1-911369-48-6
eBook edition: ISBN 978-1-911369-49-3

Second edition

Series editor: Maurice Claypole

A CIP catalogue record for this book is available from the British Library.

LinguaBooks
Elsie Whiteley Innovation Centre
Hopwood Lane
Halifax HX1 5ER
United Kingdom

www.linguabooks.com

"The best thing for being sad," replied Merlin [...] "is to learn something. That's the only thing that never fails. You may grow old and trembling in your anatomies, you may lie awake at night listening to the disorder of your veins, you may miss your only love, you may see the world about you devastated by evil lunatics, or know your honour trampled in the sewers of baser minds. There is only one thing for it then — to learn. Learn why the world wags and what wags it. That is the only thing which the mind can never exhaust, never alienate, never be tortured by, never fear or distrust, and never dream of regretting. Learning is the only thing for you. Look what a lot of things there are to learn."

— T.H. White, The Once and Future King

About the author

Andrew R. Webster holds a degree in Psychology and Philosophy from the University of Dundee and an MSc in TESOL from Edinburgh University.

Having worked in sectors as diverse as banking and social services before embarking on a career in teaching, Andrew has always been passionate about travelling to new, far flung and exciting places and immersing himself in their cultures whilst learning about their history. In keeping with this, he has taught English to a variety of different learners in countries such as Japan and South Korea, where he was based at the time of writing, providing him with a wonderful opportunity to develop the skills and knowledge required to teach different levels of English to those with varying learning abilities. His ongoing thirst for knowledge provides him with the motivation to continually explore and discover new possibilities and new philosophical approaches.

He is especially keen to investigate new teaching methods and enjoys the continuing challenges associated with the teaching of English as a second language. In particular, this involves exploring the pedagogical potential of online learning and the exploitation of virtual worlds in English language teaching.

Abstract

This work explores the role of the e-moderator, taking account of the skills required and the processes involved in creating and teaching an online English as a Foreign Language (EFL) course. It also details those theories which are applicable to online learning and how they are represented through various models, thus creating a framework to assist the e-moderation process.

In particular, Salmon's five-stage model (2004) is analysed to assess its effectiveness in helping to prepare a new e-moderator to teach in an online environment. Qualitative self-study research is conducted involving an analysis of the e-moderator's reflective journal. This method can be particularly insightful, uncovering the e-moderator's beliefs, perceptions and challenges encountered throughout the process. Thus, in-depth data is collected and used in evaluating an approach to e-moderation. It reveals how Salmon's five-stage model and others can be considerably helpful, although not sufficient in themselves, for successful online teaching and learning. In this regard, a critical appraisal and detailed analysis of Salmon's model relating to this research is conducted to assess the skills required to become a successful e-moderator.

This research reveals not only the complexities, problems, responsibilities and challenges encountered but also the tremendous rewards that can be reaped from the e-moderation process. Such research can encouragingly provide other practitioners with a valuable insight into the process and leads to recommendations for further research.

In conclusion, it is apparent that systematic frameworks such as Salmon's five-stage model can be extremely useful for effective scaffolding, but on their own they are not sufficient to produce a successful e-moderation process. It is suggested, therefore, that additional support and continual encouragement should be provided to motivate and engage students in both synchronous and asynchronous interactions. Moreover, consideration should be given to specific pedagogy and sociocultural factors when designing and implementing an online language course.

CONTENTS

Foreword

It is an intrinsic feature of human nature that we tend to view time in terms of defined periods and eras, that we prefer cut-and-dried distinctions between concepts to vague definitions and rough taxonomy. This applies to many fields of study but especially to the humanities and social sciences. We give names to historical movements, to ideas and technical innovations, thus neatly defining their existence. In terms of English language teaching, this applies especially to methodologies and peda-gogical approaches which have been variously defined, for example, as 'grammar-translation', 'direct method', 'task-based learning', 'communicative language teaching' and so on, but also to technological opportunities and the phases associated with them, such as 'pre-internet', 'computer-aided', 'online distance learning', 'web-based', 'virtual learning' and 'computer mediated communication'. In reality, however, the boundaries between such notions are far from clear; they are constantly shifting and redefining themselves and what may seem innovative from one point of view is often highly traditional when viewed from another perspective – or in some cases, vice versa. The status of online learning in general and in particular of Second Life as a platform for language teaching is a case in point. Over many years of giving talks and publishing articles on the use of virtual worlds in English Language Teaching, I have seen opinions shift and change, generally soften and in some cases harden, but for many teachers, the jury is still out.

There is no definitive work on the utility of digital technologies or on the pedagogical benefits of virtual worlds, and many commentators take a global view of what, in theory, can be done and what can not. I find it extremely refreshing, therefore, to be able to introduce through the present book an author who takes an in-depth look at a very specific aspect of online learning and language teaching.

Andrew Webster's careful and insightful study casts new light on the thoughts and aspirations of the participants in an online English class with a particular focus on the key role played by the e-moderator and the incorporation of Second Life sessions into the teaching strategy. And above all, he does so not from the point of view of an advocate of any particular approach or methodology but from that of an involved, dedicated teacher and researcher with an objective, enquiring mind, documenting his discoveries, fears and aspirations in a reflective blog.

The resulting work is not only a well-researched academic paper but also a highly personal response to one of the most daunting challenges facing today's educational community – how best to harness the language teaching potential of specific web-based technologies in an increasingly socially distanced world.

Although direct language teaching has ceased to be a common feature of Second Life since the first edition of this book appeared, the study itself has lost none of its relevance. The author's observations on online teacher-student interaction remain valid regardless of the chosen platform. Furthermore, software developers and service providers have considerably narrowed the gap between the real world and a plurality of virtual reality platforms, thus increasing the potential of such technologies for both teachers and learners. In short, a lot has been learned, but there is still much to discover.

Maurice Claypole BA, MA (Lond), Cert Ed, MCIL, MCollT, AITI, PhD
January 2022

Acknowledgements

The opportunity to conduct research and write the dissertation on which this book is based was a rewarding and challenging experience. Such an opportunity would not have been possible without continual commitment and support from the following people, whom I would like to take this opportunity to thank. Firstly, this research would have been impossible to conduct without the enthusiastic and hard-working participants on my online course and also the advice and encouragement from an online Personal Learning Network. Secondly, my family and friends have constantly provided me with determination and understanding throughout the process. Both my father and mother have been a continual source of motivation and positivity throughout. Additionally, the MSc TESOL staff in Moray House provided me with inspiration throughout my year at Edinburgh University. They gave me the necessary scaffolding and encouragement to produce assignments and provided me with the skills and knowledge required to complete the original dissertation. In particular, I would like to thank my tutor, Ruby Rennie, for assisting me with guidance and reassurance throughout. Also, I would like to thank my partner Susan Gowans, who tolerated all my stresses and anxieties. She has given me an immense amount of support and encouragement throughout this valuable experience. Finally, I would like to thank Maurice Claypole of LinguaBooks for encouraging me to make this work available to a wider audience by publishing it in book form.

Chapter 1: Introduction

1.1. *Rationale*

The purpose of this study is to consider the skills necessary and theories required to teach language learners within a fully online learning environment. A pivotal reason for carrying out such research was the observation of a continuing and heated debate on the potential for using technology to learn English (IATEFL, 2011). Hockly (2011), states that more research is required into the effectiveness of Computer Aided Language Learning (CALL), and she affirms that it is not the technology itself, but rather how it is used, which can impact on learning. According to Salmon (2011: ix), "Successful online learning depends on teachers and trainers acquiring new competencies, on their becoming aware of its potential and on inspiring the learners, rather than on mastering technology." Hockly (2011: n.p.) emphasises that "more rigorous research into ICT [Information and Communications Technology] use is needed to be able to assess impacts on language abilities." In addition, Thornbury (2011) indicates the potential for the use of technology in learning, but remains sceptical of its effectiveness. He explains that technology provides an overwhelming amount of accessible information and that technological tools are created daily and championed as ways to support learning. This can certainly be very beneficial, but only if pedagogical principles determine the use of such tools and using technology can only be justified if utilised appropriately. The research carried out here adds substance to this debate and encourages other EFL teachers to conduct similar research.

After developing an online course (see Appendix 1), it is beneficial to see how it would actually work in practice. Salmon's five-stage model (see Appendix 3), was used as a framework for the design of the online course, to provide scaffolding for the e-moderation process alongside the e-moderator's use of a reflective journal (see Appendix 2). This was then analysed by the researcher leading to the production of effective data. This research will be beneficial not only to EFL teachers interested in teaching online, but also to those already familiar with this environment. It is advantageous in the development of personal practice whilst reinforcing the benefits of online learning. The research critically evaluates Salmon's five-stage model in an attempt to analyse its suitability as an effective framework to assist practitioners wishing to pursue a similar experience outside the classroom. An online environment provides flexible learning, where students can connect with learners globally and are enabled to learn at their own pace. This exploratory study evaluates my first experience of teaching online, and the impact Salmon's five-stage model had on my practice and development. The research supports the claim that "teaching online is not the future anymore. It is an important part of the here and now of language teaching education. Teachers need to know what tools are out there and what techniques can help them use these tools" (Hockly and Clandfield, 2010: 3). An outline of the work is presented in this chapter.

Chapter Two – *Literature review* – provides an outline of the theories applicable to learning online and demonstrates their integration into e-learning models, which are used as a framework to scaffold the e-moderation process. A detailed analysis of the e-Learning ladder (Moule, 2007), skills pyramid (Hample and Stickler, 2005) and, in particular, Salmon's (2004) five-stage model, will all be presented to emphasise the complexity of skills necessary and scaffolding required for successful e-moderation. It is beneficial for this specific study – which provides a theoretical understanding and an informed basis for the skills required to teach effectively online – to focus on current research and the particular models mentioned.

Chapter Three – *Data collection* – details the context of this research and demonstrates the appropriateness of conducting qualitative, self-study research whilst emphasising the advantages of utilising a reflective journal as a beneficial method of collecting data. It is explained that such a methodology not only provides new understandings and insight into the e-moderation process, but points towards informing pedagogy and to developing and transforming practice.

This is further illuminated in Chapter Four – *Analysis and results*. Analysis of the reflective journal was carried out and a focus on the specific research questions forms the basis of categories, e.g. 'teacher's role', which assists in uncovering and explaining what occurred. Thus, the e-moderator's beliefs, perceptions and challenges encountered are disclosed and a detailed analysis of the findings in relation to Salmon's five-stage model is discussed. Revisiting Salmon's model is considered necessary to evaluate its effectiveness during this research. The benefits of such an analysis are thereafter outlined and a greater understanding of the e-moderation process is therefore achieved.

Finally, in Chapter Five – *Discussion and conclusion* – the research is connected to and compared with the theories and models explained in the Literature Review. The effectiveness of these models is revealed in relation to this particular study. Furthermore, the strengths and weaknesses of this research are discussed, leading to a proposition for further research opportunities.

1.2. *Research questions*

The following questions were addressed in the context of teaching in an online environment and provided a purpose and focus for the research:

- Does Salmon's five-stage model adequately prepare an e-moderator for the complexity of an online language learning environment?
- What is the teacher's role in an online learning environment?
- What challenges does an e-moderator face when teaching online for the first time?
- What are the e-moderator's beliefs and perceptions about teaching within an online language learning environment?

Chapter Two outlines the literature which will provide the necessary background knowledge and understanding to assist in addressing these specific questions.

Chapter 2: Literature review

2.1. Introduction

A wide variety of literature is available relating to the challenges to be faced and strategies required for effective online teaching (Beetham and Sharpe, 2007; Conceicao, 2007; Pachler and Daly, 2011; Vlachopoulos and Cowan, 2010). Such literature acknowledges what positive effects technology can have on pedagogy and suggests many ways to improve practice and to support the learning experience through the introduction of effective design and appropriate, informed activities. Unfortunately, they do not specifically address the issue of what skills are needed to teach successfully online, accentuating instead the gaps in the literature. Nevertheless, Hample and Stickler (2005) emphasised the need to address what approaches and skills are required, whilst Compton (2009: 96) acknowledged the complexity of identifying the necessary skills concluding that "more research needs to be done to identify these skills and responsibilities". Further research has also shown that an effective online learning environment can be enhanced by the e-moderator creating and maintaining a supportive online learning community (Goodfellow and Lamy, 2009; Senior, 2010). "Teachers must learn to recognise the social processes that technology enables and understand how to support these processes as a way to foster the emergence of meaningful communities" (Wenger, 2009: 191). In accordance with the current research, this literature review will describe the various theories which relate to learning online. It will provide a detailed analysis of three models which incorporate these theories along with the skills needed to teach effectively online. The comparison of such models is necessary in order to highlight their strengths and weaknesses and to analyse whether they can provide helpful scaffolding for new e-moderators.

2.2. *Computer-mediated communication*

Advances in technology have led to greater opportunities for the online learning process. Although some teachers still use technology to support a teacher-centred approach, the dynamics of this exciting and innovative environment now make it possible for teachers to change their pedagogy towards a largely student-centred approach. This type of approach provides an effective alternative to the more traditional teacher-centred practice with the introduction of more interactive and collaborative Web 2.0 tools which, if used properly, can create more meaningful and communicative tasks, where peer interaction becomes a necessary activity. Carr (2010: 117) agrees with this, stating that "The net's interactivity gives us powerful new tools for finding information, expressing ourselves, and conversing with others." It is, however, important not to rely on these tools for effective learning; they should rather be used wisely in tandem with pedagogical skills:

> Online teaching is as much about creating, communication, support and interactions as classroom teaching is: we still have the teacher, the students, the language. The main difference is that the all-important human elements are mediated by machines. (Hockly and Clandfield, 2010: 31)

When developing tasks, the teacher should think carefully about the most effective way to stimulate and engage student interaction and along with this encourage student centred learning (Lave and Wenger, 1991; Pritchard, 2007). Accordingly, learners need to become aware of their responsibilities during the learning process. By the introduction of a variety of group tasks and enabling access to a wealth of information from online sources, students can develop individually whilst at the same time benefiting from interaction with peers. This provides a catalyst for development of the construction of collaborative learning. Murugaiah and Thang (2010: 23) acknowledge that "it is evident that for online learning to benefit ESL students, it must incorporate social interaction, collaboration and reflection."

The co-construction of knowledge through collaboration relates to the Social Constructivist Theory (Vygotsky, 1978). According to this theory, learning does not occur in isolation but rather from interaction with others. Designing an online course should adhere to these constructivist principles, which encourage opportunities for meaningful collaboration between students. This enables them to reflect on their own ideas and how these compare with those of others. Learning within such a social environment is essential for an effective learning experience (Adams, 2006).

2.3. Theories of learning online

There are many advantages of learning online. It provides a suitable platform for language learning, where communicative and authentic tasks can be implemented within an environment where different cultures can interact and create meaning (O'Dowd, 2007). In addition, the use of Web 2.0 tools makes it possible to stimulate and encourage collaborative intercultural communication, where learning occurs through active participation within a supportive community. In acknowledging the benefits of online learning, Warschauer and Kern (2000) emphasise that learner-centred and communicative learning are highly suited to an online environment. This is very much in accordance with the sociocultural and social constructivist approaches to learning. The constructivist and connectivist theories of learning, as well as communities of practice, relate to face-to-face contexts but nevertheless are particularly suitable for teaching and learning online. Constructivist theory views knowledge as socially constructed instead of being transmitted (Richards and Rodgers, 2001). Adopting a learner-centred approach, the teacher focuses on the experience which students bring to a particular situation and empowers them to build on this by paying particular attention to individual needs and aspirations. Pegrum (2009) explains that through active collaboration, students engage in authentic and dynamic interaction, depending on each other to successfully complete tasks together. In addition, Felix (2002: 12) explains that the constructivist approach to learning is well suited to the affordances of the internet, because of the "potential to engage students in real experiential learning with exposure to meaningful, goal-orientated activities in authentic settings." In support of, and closely linked to this approach, connectivity as proposed by Siemens (2004) is also considered necessary for a sense of community to develop. Because of the physical separation experienced in learning online, it is even more essential to establish a social presence in order to avoid isolation and dislocation.

Rovai (2002) also considers connectivity, stating that it relates to the strength of social cohesiveness and integration created, which depends on nurturing and development of relationships within a supportive environment. Whether face–to-face or online, the teacher's role should take account of the development and maintenance of connections, to ensure the most effective ways to influence and support learning. An online course will not foster connectivity and social constructivism on its own, but rather both teacher and students are required to supportively maintain and develop a sense of community together. Communities of practice (CoPs) as defined by Wenger (1998) are exemplified by a dynamic and meaningfully engaged community, where learning is mutually constructed together within a shared context. CoPs provide a platform for self-expression and, at the same time, collaboration within supportive groups creating a multitude of learning partners. The internet provides an environment to form communities without boundaries, accessible around the world regardless of differing time zones. Wenger (2009) suggests that the e-moderator should also adopt the role of technological steward, to assist in facilitating the learning within a community. This role requires the selection of appropriate tools suitable to the community's interests, whilst at the same time recognising the constraints of technology and the tolerance of the community in using specific tools. Despite these technological concerns, Wenger (2009: 185) emphasises the potential of the internet to "enable the formation of communities we could never have imagined before." Dudeney and Hockley (2007: 152) assert that "using software that actively encourages the development of COP further enhances the social constructivist nature of the learning taking place."

There is a great deal of research on the theories used to learn effectively online; however, there seems to be less focus on how the tutor develops their teaching practice online and whether such practice clashes with our own assumptions and pedagogical beliefs. In response to this, O'Dowd (2009) accentuates the need for further research into the experiences of the e-moderator. Senior (2010: 146) asserts that teachers should widen their conceptualisation of practice and realise that online teaching requires a complexity of roles, because "if they continue to define their roles narrowly, teachers will find themselves increasingly marginalised in the rapidly-changing educational landscape of the 21st century." The role of facilitator is considered a necessity when teaching online. This raises the question of what should be done if the tutor's facilitation is ineffective, and what other roles should be considered to teach effectively online.

There have been several attempts to address these questions. The early identification of roles required to support and develop learning considered cognitive, social and pedagogic facilitation (Berge, 1995). Later Salmon (2004) proposed a more modest role for the e-moderator which does not require responsibilities associated with tutoring, or even expert knowledge of the subject matter. This role rather views the e-moderator as a facilitator of online discussion and a 'guide on the side' as described by Collinson et al. (2000). In contrast, Garrison and Anderson (2003) assert that the e-moderator's role holds more responsibility, in encouraging interactive opportunities towards achieving learning outcomes. They further assert that the online environment cannot replicate the same skills that are employed when teaching face-to-face but advise that other skills are needed to teach in such an environment. Vlachopoulos and

Cowan (2010) however, suggest that the skills needed to teach language online are similar to those employed in face-to-face classroom situations. Earlier studies by Oliver and Shaw (2003) and Aviv et al. (2003) asserted that there was a significant improvement in online discussion when the e-moderator influenced and guided students to engage. Further studies have emphasised that the e-moderator's role does not just involve support, but also requires an active and challenging stance, with high levels of involvement in fostering adequate interaction amongst students (Oliveira et al., 2011; Oncu and Cakir, 2011). Conceicao (2007: 6) affirms that "online instructors may take on a variety of roles depending on the tasks performed during the design and delivery of the online course and influenced by learner characteristics, content and course environment." From these studies, Vlachopoulos and Cowan (2010: 214) "suggest that the design and facilitation of online discussions should recognize that interaction does not just happen, but must be intentionally designed into the task and its facilitation". Furthermore, they state that studies need to be conducted to research the impact of different types of facilitative intervention and to recognise how tutors develop whilst teaching online and notice what support is required during the process.

To assist the teacher in the task of teaching online, there are several helpful models of learning to draw upon including Salmon's five-stage model, the e-learning ladder and the skills pyramid. The following sections will outline these three models, detailing the underlying theories, analysing the similarities and differences of each, and their appropriateness for the e-moderation of an online language learning course.

2.4. *Salmon's five-stage model*

Salmon's (2004) five-stage model (see Appendix 2) provides a structured framework which incorporates the Constructivist Theory, providing necessary scaffolding to support the e-moderator in developing and enabling successful learning amongst students. Adopting such a model will assist in giving adequate guidance to teachers, so that they can become more aware of the stages encountered throughout the process of online learning. It emphasises the realisation that learning online is a social process, essentially requiring collaborative activities which are skilfully initiated and moderated by the teacher.

E-tivities (Salmon, 2002) are designed in accordance with each stage of the model and these should both motivate and engage students to interact and contribute to an online community. During the process, the e-moderator must evaluate student participation whilst stimulating conversation, summarising interaction and generating constructive feedback. Furthermore, it is essential that the moderator responds quickly to student messages and ensures that anyone not participating is contacted directly and provided with necessary support. It is important to identify problems which could be encountered during this process.

First, students need to be able to access the course online and it is essential that students are made aware of the technological requirements before starting the course. Beginning any course can be difficult and certainly any problems with technology can lead to frustration, which can be alleviated by providing students with adequate technical support to enable their participation.

Secondly, students within the group may be at different stages in their development and as such, the e-moderator needs to cater for a wide range of abilities. The overall philosophy of the course and the design of e-tivities can considerably impact on how students develop throughout the process. Salmon's model is more concerned with an asynchronous environment, focusing on interaction and using easily accessible platforms such as online forums. Its central themes and methodology can nevertheless be used as a framework to assist a more blended environment, using a variety of tools in order to stimulate meaningful communication. It is evident that this model is very effective in supporting online communication of a variety of different professions. However, it is uncertain whether it can effectively be adapted to support an online language learning community and it gives no indication of what time is required to complete each stage. In addition, its linearity seems to be restrictive, in that it does not take into consideration the implications of using a variety of platforms, or of introducing new tools throughout the developmental process.

Salmon's popular model remains a dominant framework in demonstrating a coherent, process based model for teaching and learning online. Employing a constructivist approach, it takes into account the learner's participation and the e-moderator's role in facilitating learning and technical skills required throughout the stages. In objectifying such a model, it can easily be adapted to aid the design of online learning environments, often without considering particular contexts and learning styles. This oversight can be detrimental and as such the rigidity of its linear structure should not be overlooked. Practitioners need to be very careful in the reification of such a model (Lisewski and Joyce, 2003). Furthermore, the restrictive design of the model can prove to be ineffectual in long-term usage. As it has been exclusively designed for a fully online environment, it remains inflexible when applied to a blended environment. Jones and Peachey (2005) adapted Salmon's model to incorporate a face-to-face element at the start of the learning process. This proved to be effective initially in assisting with access and technical issues and also encouraged and nurtured co-operation and socialisation before introducing the online asynchronous environment. Their experience highlighted that the stages in Salmon's model did not occur in a linear fashion, but rather different stages seemed to be appropriate at different times during the course.

It is therefore apparent that Salmon's model does not adapt well to a less formal context and additionally, as it does not integrate a face-to-face component, its structure appears to be inflexible and too rigid to apply directly to blended courses. Moule (2007: 39) argues that "through slavishly applying the model as a rigid course, any opportunities to develop flexibility and reflexivity are lost." In response to this, Salmon (2007) does not advocate using her model used rigidly, but instead suggests that it should be adaptable to a variety of contexts and different technologies, further asserting that it can also incorporate face-to-face learning. Moreover, in her recent edition of 'e-moderating' (2011), Salmon proves that the five-stage model can be adapted to scaffold teaching and learning in virtual worlds such as Second Life, thus illustrating the flexibility of the model (see Appendix 4).

2.5. The e-learning ladder

In a critique of the perceived weaknesses of Salmon's model, Moule (2007) created an alternative conceptual model – 'The e-learning ladder' (see Appendix 5). In acknowledgment of the diversity of learning approaches, it incorporates both instructivist and constructivist approaches to learning, along with an emphasis on forming a community of practice. Instead of a staircase of stages, this model represents a ladder analogy which offers a variety of pedagogy which can be adapted to suit a particular course. The bottom of the ladder emphasises the instructivist approach to learning, where students explore and access information using the computer to source material and aid learning. At the top of the ladder, the constructivist approach is employed, with more creative interaction and engagement in accordance with Vygotsky's sociocultural theory (1978), showing that knowledge is created through meaningful communication. Both synchronous and asynchronous forms of online communication are taken into consideration, indicating the strengths of each in stimulating communication and the creation of knowledge.

The formation of communities of practice (Wenger, 1998), sits at the top of the ladder and this can only be achieved by interaction throughout the learning process. Learning within this environment evolves with increased social interaction and a community is formed, where each participant develops individually as the group strengthens. Along with the constructivist approach, research has looked at the possibilities for development of a community of practice (CoP) in an online context. The socialisation stage in Salmon's model, which emphasises interaction and collaboration, can provide the catalyst needed to develop online communities. In analysis of online dialogue, research has shown the presence of CoP characteristics such as mutual engagement (Rogers, 2000). However, the validity of such studies is questioned because of the small sample size and also the limited period of engagements made during research. CoPs result from sustained relationships with continual interaction and sharing of information, requiring a longer period of time. Furthermore, the disparity of contexts can create difficulties for participants in developing trust and working together within a group.

The sides of the e-learning ladder indicate the support needed throughout the e-learning process. The right-hand side of the ladder acknowledges that technological and access issues are on-going. Such issues can, unfortunately, create a barrier to successful learning and, because of the increasing complexity of the online environment, can be problematic (Monteith and Smith, 2001). It is therefore essential that continuing support be maintained to nurture and develop students' ICT skills. This can be achieved by providing the necessary support needed to become confident with the technical skills required, in order to access and effectively use a variety of e-learning tools and platforms. In addition to the technical support provided, social and pedagogical support are also necessary and these are placed on the right-hand side of the ladder. Tutor facilitation should be continuous in supporting socialisation and maintaining interaction within the group (Monteith and Smith, 2001). The emergence of a community of practice will only occur if students spend sufficient time engaging in meaningful communication, whilst also developing a history together as a group. This cannot be achieved in a short time frame, as this can reflect on the environment, with participants becoming less committed to forming a rapport within the group. In addition, lack of time spent in the initial stages of interaction can prove to be detrimental and therefore extra time needs to be spent fostering collaboration within the group. In accordance with the constructivist approach, the development of cooperative relationships can lead to a positive impact on the overall group performance. Although Moule's model adapts Salmon's model to include an instructivist approach and face-to-face learning, it also adopts it as a framework which engages learners to develop towards more independent and reflective learning, whilst at the same time displaying features representing a CoP.

The tutor's role in both models remains that of a facilitator, who implements technology and intervenes appropriately. However, Moule's model asserts that this role is required consistently throughout the process, as technological problems will continue to arise and students will stay motivated by appropriate and engaging feedback. What both models do not consider, however, is what happens once learners have actually developed the required skills to learn confidently in an online environment and this should be allowed for in the future. The teacher's role in an online environment is certainly more than just that of facilitator. The teacher needs to take account of other issues including pedagogy, managerial skills, social aspects and technical competence (Maor, 2003). The tasks encountered by the teacher can be overwhelming and it would therefore be beneficial to implement team teaching, where each teacher could take responsibility for different roles and share the complex task of e-moderation. Constant monitoring and evaluation are also needed, to make sure that students are constantly interested, challenged and encouraged to focus on the tasks provided. Murugaiah and Thang (2010: 22) indicated that the tutor "has to design activities that not only engage the students productively, but are able to motivate and move them towards self-directedness."

Murugaiah and Thang's (2010) recent study demonstrated that the initial apprehension experienced by students contributing in an unfamiliar environment was slowly changed by them becoming more active in group participation. They showed that it takes time for students to adapt to an environment which does not rely on face-to-face communication, demonstrating that learning occurs when students are more relaxed and start to form a closer bond with their peers. One problem encountered with their study was that several students were unable to engage fully because of other commitments and because of sociocultural factors. They somehow felt that it might be impolite or disrespectful for them to comment on other students' posts. A communication barrier was certainly evident because of the absence of face-to-face interaction.

In order to resolve these challenges, it is important for tutors to be aware of such issues and to make sure that they are available to guide and scaffold students, whilst offering advice and attending quickly to any problems encountered. In addition, tasks should take into consideration several factors, including cultural background, group size and age of participants (Koh and Hill, 2009). Although there are certainly many challenges to be faced, the benefits of online learning more than outweigh any problems encountered.

2.6. Skills pyramid

Hampel and Stickler (2005) produced a skills pyramid in an attempt to address these challenges (see Appendix 6). The first three levels of the pyramid relate to technological requirements and also the skills required in assessing any benefits in using such applications and how they can be used to produce effective Computer Assisted Language Learning (CALL) activities. Levels Three and Four relate to online socialisation and communication. Socialisation is very dependent on meaningful interaction between participants and in establishing a sense of community. In this regard, the tutor needs to have strong communication skills in order to stimulate participation and maintain interest in the course. Furthermore, effective task design is extremely important to assist in interaction and to encourage social cohesion. The top two stages of the pyramid require use of certain skills to enable critical evaluation and appropriate selection and design of resources along with online tools which can mediate communication. Moreover, the tutor needs to understand when and how to support and encourage students with opportunities to interact. When reaching the top of the pyramid, the intention is for tutors to have acquired a variety of suitable skills required for teaching online language learning. At this stage, teachers should be able to exert their own teaching style, using skills already obtained, continuing to make the most of the resources available, whilst maintaining a strong rapport with students despite any lack of visual cues or restrictions.

Hampel and Stickler emphasised that the specific skills required to teach a language online are different from those required for other subjects or those employed within the classroom setting. Understanding how to use the technology is certainly a requirement, but in itself is not adequate and instead there should be a greater focus on pedagogy. Rather than teachers having to acquire relevant skills through their own self-study, there needs to be more explicit instruction and guidance for teachers. "Clarification of key competencies is crucial for online language teacher training, since teaching online requires skills that differ from traditional language teaching as well as teaching other subjects online" (Compton, 2009: 76).

In addition, Compton (2009) argues that the only skill specific to language learning within the skills pyramid, is that required to facilitate communication. This could therefore be used as a framework for different teaching contexts, being not necessarily only applicable to language learning. Furthermore, she states that the sequential nature of the pyramid is problematic, as some stages of the pyramid occur concurrently and higher stages may actually be obtained before lower skill levels. In addition, it is not made clear when the teacher will become competent with the necessary skills and be ready to put them into practice.

In response to this, Compton developed a framework (see Appendix 7) which would instead address only the main skills specific to teaching an online language learning course. The three key skills in this model are technology, pedagogy and evaluation, with levels of expertise attached to each, ranging from novice to proficient and finally expert. The technology skills relate to the teacher's familiarity and understanding of the affordances of technology in relation to online language learning. Being able to identify and evaluate the pros and cons of CMC technologies, whilst showing awareness of the differences between synchronous and asynchronous communication, is an essential skill needed in determining the most suitable software required to assist tasks. "The proficient teacher is capable of drawing on the software's existing features to facilitate the language learning process including content delivery, online interactions and course management" (Compton, 2009: 83). The pedagogical skills relate to the knowledge of strategies and theories used to facilitate communicative language learning, develop communities and foster a learner-centred environment to encourage negotiation of meaning and cultural sensitivity. This can be achieved by providing clear instructions, encouraging interaction, mediating communication and providing purposeful and engaging task-based activities (Willis and Willis, 2007). The evaluative skills section relates to the importance of conducting continual formative evaluation, to determine whether desired outcomes are achieved.

Along with these three skill areas, Compton also provides a detailed description of the tutor's responsibilities, asserting that the tutor should support and motivate students to actively participate, and try to increase their confidence with more self-directed learning. A successful online learning experience can be ensured, through encouraging students to increase their responsibility for more autonomous learning (Benson, 2007), whilst providing sufficient opportunities for them to meaningfully interact (White, 2003). In order for the tutor to fully understand the challenges encountered and realise the strategies and skills required to teach effectively online, it is extremely beneficial for them to personally experience what it is like to interact and learn online from a learner's perspective. Certainly, developing the necessary skills and techniques to facilitate socialisation and the building of a community can be challenging and tutors need to be prepared with a variety of skills for any difficulties which may arise. "More research needs to be done to identify these skills and responsibilities so that language teacher preparation programmes can continue to improve and serve the needs of future online language teachers" (Compton, 2009: 96). Having duly investigated the current literature available and identified the particular skills and features required this can greatly assist future practitioners to improve their teaching practice in an online environment. Furthermore, this literature review has provided the reader with the necessary knowledge and insight into current research relating to this particular study. The next chapter gives a detailed account of the context and specific methodology used to conduct this research.

Chapter 3: Data collection

3.1. Research method and design

The design and approach used in the analysis and collection of data is largely dependent on the specific questions posed (Thomas, 2009). As mentioned in Chapter One the following questions were addressed in the context of teaching in an online environment and provided a purpose and focus for the research:

- Does Salmon's five-stage model adequately prepare an e-moderator for the complexity of an online language learning environment?
- What is the teacher's role in an online learning environment?
- What challenges does an e-moderator face when teaching online for the first time?
- What are the e-moderator's beliefs and perceptions about teaching within an online language learning environment?

This study documented the introspective reflections of an e-moderator during a one-month pilot online course for language learners. It took into account the interactions and challenges which were encountered throughout the process. The researcher's reflective thoughts were analysed with the benefit of previous experience, knowledge and theory, based on Salmon's five-stage model. The data produced should provide insight into developing future practice; however, because of the overall subjectivity of this particular research, there were no attempts to make generalisations, but positive suggestions were made to improve future practice.

Researching educational practice from the perspective of an outsider who is not directly involved with the teaching practice can be very challenging, because of the complexity of interactions and specific environmental constraints. There are many elements to take into consideration which may cause difficulties. For instance, a great variety of learner beliefs and perceptions can influence the study of interactions within an educational environment. The research did not account for an outsider's perspective, which could be considered as a limitation, therefore becoming a more subjective account. In this regard, Pring (2004: 123) acknowledged that the "privileged position of the teacher in educational research raises questions about the objectivity and impartiality of the researcher". However, the researcher valued such a position and decided to adopt the role of the e-moderator, thus gaining a more personal insight into the e-moderation process.

Research was carried out over a four-week period and involved the teaching of seven EFL students on an online language learning course. A purposive sample of students was chosen to meet the course requirements. They were of an intermediate/advanced level of English, lived in a target language removed context and had an average age of twenty-eight. The sample consisted of one Mexican, one Japanese, one Taiwanese, three Chinese and one German student. Differing nationalities were specifically chosen to emphasise the global aspects of learning online. This was a new and meaningful experience not only for the e-moderator but also for the students involved. In accordance with the BERA (2004) guidelines, necessary steps were taken to ensure that all participants fully understood the purpose of the research process. Although the e-moderator was the only participant in this self-study research, there was still a requirement to make sure that students were informed of the nature of research, in the unlikely event that their privacy was put at risk. Therefore, before the course started, the students were made aware of the requirements of the research project, including the length of the course and their right to withdraw during the process (Mann and Stewart, 2000). Students were also informed of technological necessities and requirements in order to participate in the course. Following this, consent was given by participants for any relevant information produced during the course to be later used as data. Such data was then stored securely and if published in future, students were informed that anonymity would be assured to protect their privacy. Because the research was conducted online, the privacy of participants was a particularly important ethical issue for consideration (Thurlow, et al., 2004). Thus the online course was made private and confidential, only accessible to the e-moderator and students. Furthermore, the e-moderator's online diary did not disclose any students' names. According to Bruckman (2002), the manner of consent obtained online depends on the research conducted. Therefore, because of the low levels of risk to students in this research, they were only informed electronically via email and consent was also given by this means. Conducting such research certainly informed the researcher's own practice, challenged assumptions and high-lighted the complexity of teaching and learning in an online environment (Mitchell et al., 2005).

Self-study was the chosen methodology for this research with the underlying purpose of reflecting on and scrutinising the relationship between the complexity of practice and theory, with a view to improving practice and developing new understandings. Loughran and Russell (2002: 227) assert that self-study is "about rediscovering the relationship between theory, practice and research, in a way that is more connected to, and reflective of, one's professional life" and this was the intention. In addition, the research conducted was contextually bound and focused on a single perspective. It proved to be challenging, highlighting personal difficulties in confronting and assessing flaws which were revealed in personal practice. This revelation prompted real insight and provided powerful, positive data.

Self-study has proved to be an advantageous methodology for researchers wanting to understand and improve their own teaching practice, whilst at the same time providing meaningful insights for other practitioners (Clandinin and Connelly, 2004). Adopting this form of methodology seemed highly appropriate for the purpose of this particular research. Valuing the individual voice and personal thoughts of the researcher in relation to their own situation offers invigorating and rigorous research which can generate an insightful articulation of the theories and assumptions governing the researcher's own practice (Tidwell, 2002). Such methodology requires integrity and responsibility to be shown by the researcher and the researched. Placing the 'self' in this position can assist in gaining a depth of understanding on how beliefs and theories of teaching can differ when they are actually translated into practice. Paying particular attention to the actions performed within the present moment of practice can reveal and assist in exploring and making more explicit the tacit knowledge brought to the situation which informs the actions (Clandinin and Connelly, 2000, 2004).

Uncovering and documenting this awareness helped in reforming knowledge, refining practice and should also benefit and guide other practitioners in changing their own practice.

Self-study, however, not only gives an insight into the 'self' but relies on interactions with others in confirming assumptions and interpretations. Pinnegar and Hamilton (2009: 20) explain that "although messy and contingent, working to articulate, alter, and understand these relationships, holds great potential for producing knowledge, actions and understandings that will allow practitioners to develop better practices." Collaborating and drawing on others as critical friends is an important part of this chosen method of self-study. At the start of the research process therefore, other EFL practitioners were consulted for suggestions and advice on how to improve the online course and provide hints and tips for effective teaching online. Developing an online PLN (Personal Learning Network) was extremely beneficial, providing encouragement and support throughout the initial stages of research. As described by Hockly and Clandfield (2010: 108), a PLN "refer[s] to the way we integrate many sources of information and communication into our personal and professional development." Adoption of this methodology stems from the researcher's curiosity in understanding and learning more about teaching online and, in addition, whether employing a self-designed course in accordance with Salmon's five-stage model could successfully translate into practice. There was also a desire to explore and illuminate what tensions, as well as successes, would be encountered when teaching within a fully online environment. The hope was that this whole process would provide new possibilities and, at the same time, enhance personal experience through using an online course, whilst identifying whether personal beliefs, theoretical understandings and assumptions actually occur in reality.

Undergoing such research requires a very critical stance in uncovering and gaining insights into assumptions and influences which determine practice. In addition, the identification and examination of beliefs about teaching can assist in responding to, changing and potentially transforming current practice (LaBosky, 2004). With a central focus on the 'self' in relation to the complex nature of teaching, this whole process can prove to be a daunting task. Adopting such an insider's perspective could, possibly, appear to be a self-indulgent exercise but its main concern was to uncover an understanding of our teaching practice and its effects on students' learning. Thus the "focus while apparently on the teacher 'self', is *always* on the student and how to create a meaningful learning environment" (Coia and Taylor, 2009: 16).

Methods chosen to collect data are varied and are dependent on the context being studied. The teacher's natural environment is the most appropriate setting to learn and enquire about the nature of their teaching whilst gaining a more reflective insight into such a particular environment. This can also assist in providing a clearer understanding of the context. In addition, the teacher's previous personal experience along with the social context could have an influence on actions made, whilst practice is continually being adjusted, depending on the needs of the students. This became more apparent when reflecting on the process.

The collection of data was designed to capture a comprehensive and coherent account representative of the research undertaken and assisted in providing evidence for the questions posed. Instead of relying purely on memory to reflect after the learning process occurred, the data was strengthened by recording the actual moment of practice as it happened, which was then reconsidered and evaluated in light of further inquiry. It is the responsibility of teachers to remain open minded throughout the process and to modify practice in accordance with new knowledge obtained, through continually scrutinising practice and challenging assumptions. Loughran (2004) observed that an essential aspect of self-study is to share the interpreted data publicly to encourage diversity of opinion which will evaluate the findings and thereby gain further understanding of practice. In this regard, making the journal available by using an online blog, made it available to share with a global community of educational practitioners. The method for collecting data involved the e-moderator maintaining a regular journal of the whole process. The blog (see Appendix 2) was created to document relevant and important information, events and reflection prior to, and throughout, the four-week course. Keeping a journal certainly required commitment and consistent effort, which proved to be very time consuming, as noted by Bell (2010). In order for this to work effectively, the e-moderator allocated strict and regular times to write entries in the journal. Any revealing interactions with students were noted to strengthen the findings. Keeping a reflective journal provided the researcher with the opportunity to articulate and reflect on the actions taken and feelings may be expressed as they occur during the teaching-learning process. Recording not only successful occurrences, but also the frustrations and problems encountered throughout, provided fruitful insights leading to a greater awareness of current practice. With greater attention to a specific situation, it was possible to obtain a clearer view of what is usually overlooked or avoided during day-to-day practice. Effective and purposeful journaling exposed the unique perspectives of the 'self' in relation to the teaching context and captured the feelings and reflections of the experiences during practice (Cochran-Smith and Lytle, 1993; Rager, 2005). As Kitchen (2009: 48) stated, it was apparent that using journals as a research method proved to be "valuable as artefacts for retrospectively interpreting patterns in experience in order to develop deeper insights into one's practice."

As previously stated, there are no attempts to make generalised claims about knowledge, but rather more focus was placed on ontology in relation to exploring experience towards developing and understanding practice as purported by Feldman (2003). Pinnegar and Hamilton (2009: 65) expand on this, stating that "the orientation of self-study researchers toward ontology animates all aspects of our work as a guide for our study and as a commitment to developing environments that support human flourishing" and this influenced the approach taken. Denzin and Lincoln (2005) are also persuasive in noting that self-study is far removed from making claims about the uncertainty of knowledge associated with logical positivism. In preference to this, the epistemological stance has a constructivist approach to knowledge, where understandings are specifically related to particular contexts, time and the interaction within that space. As such, it was imperative to make visible the context which constrains and shapes practice. Self-study aims to question and explore alternative interpretations in the process of constructing meaning and reframing practice. In doing so, it seeks to appeal to the trustworthiness and rigour associated with the qualitative research community (Lincoln and Guba, 1985; Miles and Huberman, 1984, Mishler, 1990). It cannot be fully considered research until it has been made public and open to critique. Therefore, value and trustworthiness are open to the interpretation of the reader in accordance with their own beliefs, who determines whether the researcher acted with rigour and integrity in their assertions and provided convincing evidence of their claims.

3.2. Context

The research conducted explored the e-moderator's role, beliefs and challenges encountered during the moderation of a one-month online course. In carrying out this particular self-study, not only did I practice as researcher but also as e-moderator and will therefore, for the duration of this research, refer to myself in these terms throughout. The online course – 'Global Imaginarium' (see Appendix 1), was created for intermediate/advanced English as a Foreign Language (EFL) learners who, because of their busy lifestyles, were otherwise unable to practice their English in a classroom setting. The design of this course was to enable students to practice their English language skills in an engaging and interactive environment, suited to their own time schedule. Such an environment provides the stimulating opportunity to interact with learners from other cultures, where distance is not an issue. According to Lankshear and Knobel (2006), learning within an online environment has the possibility to transcend constraints usually associated with the classroom. Having access to the internet provides a wealth of authentic and multimodal material which, if used appropriately, can produce meaningful and engaging activities. These, as indicated by Ng (2001), may be considered as both learner-centred and collaborative. The role of the e-moderator and choice of Web 2.0 tools, are particularly important for the success of the online course. This course was created in order to incorporate Web 2.0 tools specifically chosen to facilitate constructivist learning and, at the same time, provide learners with new opportunities to take control of their own learning. Moreover, whilst designing appropriate tasks, each tool was carefully selected because of its pedagogical value, taking into consideration sociocultural factors such as background knowledge, language-learning needs and individual goals. It is important to provide a brief description of each tool used and also its pedagogical value.

Skype is a popular internet phone service, making it possible to conduct free calls with other internet users. It was used in the course to offer learners an effective one-to-one synchronous support with the e-moderator. Along with Skype, blogs were used as a form of journal, creating the basis for each activity and, as described by Lankshear and Knobel (2006: 139), these should be "largely interest-driven and intended to attract readers who have the same or similar interests and allegiances." Used effectively, they have the possibility to enrich collaboration and engage learners with the opportunity to develop meaningful and authentic communication (Davies and Merchant, 2009; Mompean, 2010; Murray and Hourigan, 2008). Interaction and collegiality, which are developed through asynchronous interaction over blogs, provided necessary scaffolding before introducing Second Life. Second Life (SL), is a virtual world "populated by avatars: virtual representations of SL members, known as residents" (Rymaszewski, 2008: 6). Such a platform provides learners with the opportunity to experience synchronous discussion in a highly immersive environment (Jauregi et al., 2011). According to Campbell (2009), Second Life's experiential environment makes it a possible method of promoting constructivist learning where the students will contribute and learn from each other, thereby strengthening the group's community of practice.

Having described these Web 2.0 tools and outlined the context for this research, the next chapter will consider how effective these chosen tools were in helping the e-moderator to create an effective online learning environment. This can be achieved by analysing the data obtained from the e-moderator's reflective journal.

Chapter 4: Data analysis and results

4.1. Data analysis

This chapter details the procedure involved in analysing data obtained from the e-moderator's reflective journal and also details the method used for analysis. It is argued that qualitative data analysis is a recursive and rigorous process which can be time consuming and ambiguous, but can also be a creative and insightful experience (Marshall and Rossman, 2006). This was certainly the case with this particular research. In interpreting the qualitative data, obtained from the reflective journal (see Appendix 2), the researcher was very careful to identify personal beliefs and the theoretical position influencing data, thus attempting to reduce any selection bias (Alaszewski, 2006). Whilst it is impossible to capture everything which occurs, it can provide an insight into further understanding the personal and subjective experience of the situation. It is true that "qualitative data analysis can describe, interpret and explain, but cannot hope to reproduce the full richness of the original data" (Dey, 1993: xiii). Therefore, the important themes and categories which emerged were compared and interpreted thoroughly, in order to provide a meaningful and illuminative analysis of the data produced (Thomas, 2009). Using the constant comparative strategy as a framework, the data collected was divided into manageable units to search for patterns, themes and categories (Dey, 1993; Ryan and Bernard, 2005; Thomas, 2009). Once broken down and re-assembled, the data was made more open to provide a more meaningful representation of what actually occurred through the researcher's observations and to assist the reader to more fully understand what occurred during the research.

The resultant data was then developed so that a fresh description emerged, considering the most salient themes for the underlying concerns of this particular research. Scott and Morrision (2006: 22) support this, stating that "for qualitative data analysts, a key task is to use categorisation in order to abstract the most important feature of the educational phenomena studied from detailed, thick and complex data." From focused and continual analysis of the resultant data, inferences were made and important themes identified. In order to focus more and further narrow the search, the researcher then decided to return to the underlying concerns of this particular research and reconsidered the initial questions posed in order to provide a source for the main categories to be addressed. This was hugely helpful in assisting with analysis, and using the aforementioned questions as categories, matched convincingly with the themes which had emerged. According to Cohen et al. (2007: 468) "This is a very useful way to organise data, as it draws together all the relevant data for the exact issue of concern to the researcher, and preserves the coherence of the material."

The analysis of data uncovered the thoughts and actions embedded in practice. In the discussion that follows, there are no definitive conclusions about the suitability of Salmon's five-stage model. The discussion does, however, provide some insights which could be further developed in future research. This study, therefore, offers some suggestions for improving practice and adds to the body of knowledge related to e-learning, online language learning, and e-moderation, although it is "contextually bound, tentative, provisional and constantly open to improvement" (Pring, 2004: 137).

4.2. Teacher's beliefs and perceptions

The course was designed for EFL learners from a target-language removed context to practise English in a way which would be flexible to their needs and at the same time, not interfere with their busy lifestyles. Moreover, such learning online with students from a variety of different cultures could provide learners with the opportunity to interact with others on a global scale which would otherwise be difficult for them to achieve. In creating such a course the e-moderator took account of Salmon's five-stage model and the underlying pedagogical theories to learn successfully in an online environment. Before beginning the online course, the e-moderator's concerns were clearly evident and some of the feelings expressed may well have been similar to those felt by the students. Not only was this the first time the e-moderator had experienced teaching online but it was also the first time that the students had embarked on learning online. Therefore, it is important to consider how the self-created course would translate into practice.

At one stage the e-moderator clearly expressed some apprehension about the potential success of the course and this led to a change in direction whilst also acknowledging that "when you finish creating a new course you feel very proud of what you have achieved and tend to not be as critical as you perhaps should" (journal extract, see Appendix 8.1.). It became apparent that the e-moderator could benefit from reassurance and much needed support from an online Personal Learning Network (PLN) and this provided advice and encouragement throughout the initial stages. Through embracing online social networks such as Twitter and Facebook, the e-moderator increased the PLN and from this gained useful access to an insightful community of practitioners. This, in turn, increased the e-moderator's energy and enthusiasm, providing reassurance and helping to combat any feelings of worry and apprehension. In making the effort to contact others for reassurance and advice, the e-moderator felt that it made a difference to know that others were interested, and that the 'sense of community' encouraged continuation with the process (journal extract, see Appendix 8.2.).

Throughout the whole process there were concerns about whether students would be able to cope with the design and activities of the course and whether too many tools were utilised. These anxieties were particularly associated with technology and whether both the students and, indeed, the e-moderator were able to cope with Web 2.0 tools. More importantly, it was questioned whether they were all necessary and would effectively aid the constructivist learning required. Apprehension was also expressed about accessing the blog, understanding Second Life and using Skype. The e-moderator was concerned with whether the amount of information provided and guidance given in the course blog was perhaps too much and overwhelming. Furthermore, there were uncertainties as to how meaningful the tasks to be performed were. Although there were insecurities and fears over possible difficulties which might arise, there was also the realisation that "It [would] be an immense learning opportunity and at the end of the process [there would be a] greater insight into teaching online" (journal extract, see Appendix 8.3.).

A lack of interaction and some students regrettably dropping out of the course added to the frustration leading to the e-moderator questioning personal teaching abilities and perceptions. These considerations were offset by the realisation that students have a variety of needs and different learning styles and that the course tasks needed to be flexible in order to cater for this. The e-moderator began to understand that uncertainties and difficulties would certainly happen regularly and that the unexpected would occur. Instead of being stressed and anxious, it became more productive to 'remain calm and carry on' with the process (journal extract, see Appendix 8.4.). It was very apparent that, as the course progressed, both e-moderator and students became more relaxed with teaching and learning online and more confident in utilising the chosen Web 2.0 tools. The feeling was that the exercise had "been an insightful experience into the complex role of the e-moderator [who had truly] benefited from [the whole] process" (journal extract, see Appendix 8.5.).

4.3. Challenges

The predominant challenges encountered throughout the course related to time, technology and social-cultural factors. Time was certainly an issue for many of the students and several students decided to discontinue the course because they were too busy to participate. This was ironic as the course was very much designed to cater for busy people. Students also claimed that they found the tasks difficult to complete on time. This prompted the e-moderator to appreciate more that the students had other priorities, and could only devote a certain amount of time to the course (journal extract, see Appendix 8.6.). Time was also an issue for the e-moderator and completion of the reflective journal became a concern. Because of a busy work schedule it was difficult for the e-moderator to regularly update the journal; however, this whole process developed greater empathy for the students who were also required to write their own blog posts. Furthermore, there was pressure to ensure that the journal was effective and it was 'difficult to write a blog post' when not feeling in the best frame of mind (journal extract, see Appendix 8.7.).

The awareness that issues of time could have a serious impact on the course was further reinforced when trying to schedule synchronous meetings online to utilise tools such as Skype and SL. It became apparent that it would be problematic trying to arrange a meeting to suit students' various schedules and differing time zones. This was only made possible after careful planning and by using an online tool called 'doodle' (http://doodle.com) for creating schedules, whilst taking into consideration availability and time differences. It was not only these time issues which needed to be addressed but also internet restrictions imposed politically by certain countries along with problems associated with the poor strength of internet connection. Chinese students were regrettably unable to access YouTube videos and some web-links attached to each task. Moreover, there was constant frustration experienced when trying to access Skype and SL caused by constant problems with logging on and temperamental sound quality. This situation was particularly problematic when students tried to use the internet during busy hours, as most people in their countries were accessing the internet at the same time and this seriously interfered with their network speed.

Issues with technology were evident throughout, with worries about students' lack of experience using Web 2.0 tools. Some of the practitioners from the e-moderator's PLN advised reducing the number of tools used and also voiced concern about the challenges imposed by virtual platforms such as SL. Another suggested that the e-moderator reduce expectations and proceed to introduce students gradually to these new tools. This advice encouraged a reduction in tools used with a revision of what tasks were to be chosen, but could not address the unavoidable technical problems encountered which "hindered the progression of tasks and created unneeded frustration [in] students" (journal extract, see Appendix 8.8.). It was not only the students who suffered inconvenience, though, since the e-moderator also experienced problems with internet connectivity. There was a real concern that connections would be weak but certainly not an expectation that the e-moderator's "own connection would interfere with the course" (journal extract, see Appendix 8.9.).

When there appeared to be a lack of interaction by some students, it was difficult to know whether they were following comments made and choosing not to interact, exemplifying a term commonly known as 'lurking'. When interaction actually dried up, it was uncertain whether students were finding certain tasks more challenging and were, therefore, taking longer to complete them. Although students appeared not to be participating, there was a realisation that they could have been studiously carrying out tasks without other students or the e-moderator realising it. A further challenge was that it took some time and perseverance for students to understand how to use a blog. When one student, for example, encountered problems with publishing her posts this was resolved by the e-moderator assisting by sharing the screen over Skype and talking to her throughout the procedure. Empathy was demonstrated by stating that it must have been frustrating to "spend a long time writing a post and then not be able to publish it" (journal extract, see Appendix 8.10.).

Second Life also proved problematic. After encouraging students to explore SL, one student had an unanticipated, uncomfortable experience. The student tried to practise their English and engage with other avatars but was frequently accosted by rude and explicit comments, otherwise known as 'flaming'. The e-moderator "was naively unaware of this happening in Second Life and from this found out that there can be a problem with griefers" (journal extract, see Appendix 8.11.) who will deliberately harass others causing unpleasant situations. Dudeney and Ramsay (2009:23), explain that "griefing describes the action of disturbing other users to limit the user's ability to carry out his/her intended aims in-world." In addition, Ball and Pearce (2009: 55) point out that 'griefers' are "trouble makers in Second Life, who can orchestrate anything from harmless pranks to sustained assaults." This was something unexpected which must be considered when using the internet for learning purposes. In response to this, care was taken to ensure that a comfortable and safe environment was chosen for subsequent synchronous meetings in Second Life. With considerable support and guidance, the students found these tools to be beneficial, despite the challenges encountered.

4.4. Teacher's role

Having discussed the challenges encountered, it is now appropriate to focus on the e-moderator's role throughout the process. As previously stated, it was highly beneficial for the e-moderator to form a supportive PLN. This is possible through social networking and by opening oneself up to an encouraging online community which provides reassurance and constructive criticism. Receiving encouraging e-mails from other practitioners provided motivation and a sense of engagement. Furthermore, the e-moderator should constantly learn from this community, which exemplifies the constructivist approach to learning where the e-moderator can construct knowledge from critical friends, in order to develop personal practice. This process is therefore similar to the students' development and growth of their own particular community of practice where receiving timely feedback from the e-moderator and regular interaction with peers provides extra enthusiasm to feel connected and part of a supportive community. It was certainly apparent that it was "extremely necessary to engage with students and install a humanistic element, so that they realised that even though there [was] a cyber-barrier created there [was nevertheless] still connection and support available" (journal extract, see Appendix 8.12.).

Along with the qualities of enthusiasm and encouragement, the e-moderator always needs to be prepared for the unknown and to notice and solve problems as they occur. Challenges similar to those faced by the students are experienced and in understanding these challenges, empathy can be shown to students and reassurance provided. One example of this occurred when a student was having problems with the internet. The e-moderator had previously encountered similar problems and could therefore "empathise with feelings of detachment. In light of this, an encouraging and reassuring email was [sent which was] important" (journal extract, see Appendix 8.13.). Positivity is essential and it is important to pass this on to students and to motivate and engage with them. Moreover, task design is crucial and should therefore be well planned, resulting in purposeful and worthwhile activities to appeal to a variety of students. It is beneficial to evaluate and change tasks accordingly, remaining flexible and student-centred, depending on students' needs and expectations. Evaluation was practised throughout with, for example, the e-moderator questioning whether instructions had been understood or the purpose of a particular task appreciated.

4.5. Salmon's five-stage model

Salmon's model was used as a scaffolding to provide a structure for the course and accompany the e-moderation process. Each task was carefully designed in relation to the five stages. Before detailing how the model related to this particular research, it is helpful to revisit it and give a brief description of each stage.

The first stage in Salmon's model – Access and motivation (Salmon, 2004) – provides an introduction to the course. A welcoming message should greet students and clear instructions given on how to access the course, together with a list of requirements for participation. The e-moderator will engage with and encourage students, whilst supporting them with any technical guidance. Basic activities are initially provided to ease students into such a new and unfamiliar environment, so that they can become more comfortable and confident in proceeding. It is essential that these activities are worthwhile and enable collaboration and involvement, whilst developing comfortable usage of the technology. In addition, this stage of the model considers the apprehension and frustration which students tend to encounter when starting an online course. The teacher should, therefore, attempt to reassure and establish a rapport with students, motivating them to work together and effectively addressing any queries or technical problems.

Stage Two – Online socialisation (Salmon, 2004) – should break the ice and welcome students to their new online community. Students are informed of online etiquette and given an outline of the course. At this stage, students are encouraged to introduce themselves to the other members of the community. Both individual and group identities are developed through the sharing of opinions and ideas. Moreover, an exchange of information should establish collaborative learning and in so doing, develop trust within the group. During this stage, students are encouraged to develop a comradeship through the sharing of ideas with their peers and by exerting their online presence in an environment which increases the student's confidence in being able to interact and co-operate with others.

In Stage Three – Information exchange (Salmon, 2004) – the e-moderator encourages students to search for purposeful information, to exchange their findings with the community and to take more control of their own learning. This is made possible by students interacting with the course content and by sourcing relevant information which is then shared with their peers. In order for this to be achieved, the tutor needs to provide appropriate tasks which suit students' needs (Salmon, 2002). Such tasks should be carefully implemented by providing clear guidelines, which inform students of their roles within the task and also state what is expected of them to successfully complete it. It is important to indicate how to access and find useful information for the benefit of both themselves and the community. In addition, the e-moderator should encourage group development by prompting discussions, asking questions and summarising any findings and outcomes. Clearly structured activities should be provided which encourage engaging discussion and interactive participation. If successful, the students will become more familiar with Computer Mediated Communication (CMC) and, in so doing, gain an understanding of group dynamics and how to operate successfully as a community.

By Stage Four – Knowledge construction (Salmon, 2004) – it is of utmost importance for the teacher to support and encourage students to interact but also to contribute to the construction of knowledge (Beldarrain, 2006). There should be a constant 'buzz of discussion' amongst students, as they supportively challenge and build knowledge together. Here, the e-moderator should facilitate learning by introducing themes and by providing spark questions, with the aim of encouraging a range of views and answers for exploration and further development. Interactivity is essential, as students begin to evaluate existing resources and develop their own. If successful, this should encourage discussion to provoke critical thinking and reflection, summarising and emphasising key points.

Following this, Stage Five – Development (Salmon, 2004) – is a culmination of all the skills acquired during this process. Students should by now have the confidence to take responsibility for their own learning. They are more able to focus on and apply what they have learned towards their own needs and goals, and to reflect critically on the learning process. Both the students and the e-moderator should now be comfortable learning together in an online learning environment. The e-moderator now takes a less active stance and supports students in taking control of their own learning, encouraging self-reflection and criticality with the aim of them becoming more self-directed. Consequently, they become more responsible for their learning and so show more commitment to their own development.

The e-moderator had experience of putting into practice all the stages prior to the course commencing. Accessing and forming a PLN provided the motivation needed to socialise with encouraging practitioners, sharing information, constructing knowledge together and finally developing more confidence in the e-moderation process. Each of the five stages took effect naturally and provided an efficient and effective way to becoming comfortable in the process and feeling more secure with teaching online.

Access, motivation and socialisation occurred during the first week of the course, with students gaining access to the course blog, introducing themselves to the online community and interacting asynchronously with each other by writing short comments. Initially, the students did not appear to be spending enough time interacting together and there was a realisation that it would take time for students to socialise and that it should not be expected for this to just happen (journal extract, see Appendix 8.15.). However, it did not take too long for this to take effect, and socialisation occurred after synchronous one-to-one meetings with the e-moderator over Skype. Live communication with students online was important not only for students to express any concerns but also for the e-moderator to motivate and reassure them. "It seem[ed] that the Skype session made the course more personable and engaging due to [this] face-to-face element" (journal extract, see Appendix 8.16.). From this development their initial apprehension about using blogs to interact was replaced with enthusiasm, when they realised the benefits and, additionally, noticed that writing posts would provide a reference for others to interact with. Students expressed their personal thoughts and frustrations whilst others responded with supportive and friendly advice. They were clearly reading each other's blogs and showing an interest by writing comments and a stream of interaction occurred on each student's blog. The e-moderator was highly encouraged by this, stating that he was "delighted that students [were] engaging with each other and did not imagine it would be so productive in the first week" (journal extract, see Appendix 8.17.).

After such a positive start to the course it was surprising that there followed an absence of communication and lack of contribution from students. In despair, the e-moderator "felt that the course was starting to crumble around [his] feet and [he] searched inside for an answer [as to] why this was happening" (journal extract, see Appendix 8.18.). The answer was thankfully found once again from the one-to-one teacher-student synchronous interaction over Skype. Students appeared mostly to contribute to the course by completing tasks just before a synchronous meeting and also increased interactions with other students after such meetings. These one-to-one meetings with the e-moderator provided motivation to complete their tasks and to encourage interaction and sharing of information, with others and students started to share information thus demonstrating Stage Three of Salmon's model.

As the course progressed, and to provide further encouragement, the e-moderator constantly sent motivating emails to
students when there was less activity. Stage One of Salmon's
model was evident during every task with the e-moderator
assisting with access problems when using tools such as Skype
and Second Life. It was extremely important to provide
motivation and encouragement to engage students, since they
were constantly busy with other lifestyle demands. Planning and
preparation were also essential to make sure that the course
provided e-activities appropriate to each of Salmon's five stages.
According to Salmon (2011: 125), "teaching online needs careful
planning and preparation, otherwise the stories will continue of
e-moderators being overloaded and burnt out by the work."
Although tasks were completed using blogs, the asynchronous
interaction was not consistent and while the e-moderator tried
to encourage students it was not as successful as planned.
However, students expressed that they benefited from sharing
their thoughts and by the end of the course felt comfortable
writing blog posts. Salmon's five-stage model was most evident
when using SL for synchronous group discussion. Scaffolding
students through Task One and Two assisted students to
become comfortable with socialising online, sharing information
with each other and they started to form a community of
practice.

Students were given an induction in SL by the e-moderator prior
to the group meeting which assisted with access and motivating
students to take part in subsequent meetings. Both students
and the e-moderator expressed apprehension about the Second
Life environment, but this apprehension was thankfully replaced
by enthusiasm and positivity. The e-moderator facilitated and
managed the discussion and students appeared to share their

opinions and construct knowledge together. The e-moderator "really felt that students were very involved in the discussion and was inspired by their contributions" (journal extract, see Appendix 8.19.). This was further strengthened in the last SL meeting with the e-moderator feeling that "Second Life really injected some much-needed energy and provided a platform for students to interact synchronously in a supportive environment" (journal extract, see Appendix 8.20.). Students evidently displayed Stages Three and Four of Salmon's model and also appeared to be showing development. The e-moderator believed that "this session in Second Life was [extremely] reflective and students took more control over the process" (journal extract, see Appendix 8.21.). It was apparent that when used loosely as scaffolding for the e-moderation process, Salmon's model was an important factor in the success of the course. However, it regrettably did not fully prepare the e-moderator for the complexity of teaching online and discussion regarding this follows in the next chapter.

Chapter 5: Discussion and conclusion

5.1. Discussion

Having analysed the data obtained from the self-study research, it is now appropriate to evaluate what has been achieved, what understandings have been reached and how the findings can be used to improve future practice. Therefore, discussion will follow as to how this particular research contributes, and connects, to other research conducted within a similar field and how successfully it attempts to answer questions and issues raised in previous studies. Finally, the researcher will consider what further research is considered necessary in order to address any unresolved issues and concerns which have arisen from this study.

Without previous experience of teaching online, the e-moderator displayed anxieties, concerns and insecurities which could have affected the process. In retrospect, although models such as the e-learning ladder, skills pyramid and five-stage model (previously discussed in the literature review), can provide helpful scaffolding, they cannot fully prepare the e-moderator for the complexity of challenges faced during the e-moderation process. Having experienced first-hand the role of e-moderator it was then necessary to evaluate the various tasks undertaken, pedagogy employed, technical and personal support required and to reconsider the e-learning models in relation to this research. Salmon's five-stage model and the skills pyramid (Hample and Stickler, 2005), both suggest that learning online is a systematic and sequential process. Both models share a commonality in that they emphasise the importance of developing socialisation whilst providing adequate technical support. One outcome of this particular research is the proposal that these aspects should certainly be given appropriate and careful attention throughout, and there is an additional argument in support of Moule's (2007) e-Learning Ladder that there should be no clear linearity of individual stages. Rather, careful support and nurturing of socialisation should be a continuous process and the e-moderator needs to pay particular attention to maintaining a strong, interactive and cohesive group of participants. In order to accomplish this, the initial design of tasks and planned involvement of the e-moderator are extremely important. According to Vlachopoulos and Cowan (2010), the e-moderator needs to be heavily involved in encouraging and motivating the development of collaborative interaction between students. Sufficient technical support is required and when utilising new tools, extra time is needed for students to become more comfortable with their usage and to understand how they can effectively be used to encourage and enrich socialisation. The data produced in this research reveals the temperamental nature and inconsistencies experienced when using technology to support learning and it consequently indicates that the usage of such technology requires continual support, empathy and encouragement.

As explained, both socialisation and technology should receive continual attention, whether using synchronous or asynchronous tasks. Although Salmon's model was particularly intended to support asynchronous learning, it is also adaptable to synchronous learning, whereas Moule's e-learning ladder explicitly considers both asynchronous and synchronous learning. It is evident from this research that synchronous tasks were more collaborative and. although asynchronous tasks formed a basis for socialisation, considerably more involvement and attention were needed to stimulate asynchronous interaction. The researcher found this aspect to be of particular interest, deserving further research in order to investigate this difference more thoroughly. Salmon's model is certainly highly effective because of its adaptability; however, the e-moderator needs to understand that particular attention should be given to their own area of practice. This, unfortunately, can be neglected when concentrating entirely on Salmon's model as may have been the case in the e-moderator's practice whilst undertaking this research. In acknowledgement of this possible pedagogical neglect, Compton (2009) specifically focuses on the related pedagogy to be put into practice through providing a descriptive model detailing the necessary skills required to teach language online. Although it is not as malleable and concise as Salmon's model, it nevertheless gives more insight into the particular pedagogy required to teach online learners effectively. Perhaps future practice could benefit if this could be integrated and used in parallel with Salmon's model. Focusing explicitly on Salmon's model is not enough to foster an effective online learning experience and, as stated by Pegrum (2009: 53), "There's no substitute for well-trained educators who, through careful planning and intensive engagement with technological, pedagogical and broader issues, can maximise the educational relevance of digital technologies."

The constructivist approach to learning (Vygotsky, 1978), which emphasises a learner-centred and communicative stance, formed the basis of each task. However, the e-moderator's journal did not explicitly mention the pedagogy and theory employed and whether they were conducive to effective online learning. In hindsight, this would have been beneficial and should be considered in future research. It was, however, apparent that synchronous discussion using Second Life incorporated several opportunities for constructivism and established connectivity whilst demonstrating social interaction, collaboration and reflection. These components are specifically mentioned by Murugaiah and Thang (2010) as being essential for online learning. On the other hand, asynchronous interaction proved to be less successful in practice, therefore prompting the need for a reconsideration and evaluation of tasks which required such interaction, accounting for individual needs in order to promote more interactive and constructive learning.

The virtual learning environment and Web 2.0 tools chosen for the course are of particular importance and with reference to Wenger (2009) the e-moderator should adopt the role of tech steward in considering the constraints of using certain technologies and their appropriateness to students' needs and tolerance of usage. However, the selection and implementation of Web 2.0 tools, which should encourage discussion and emphasise the constructivist approach to learning, does not necessarily result in collaboration, as was found to be the case here. The choice and preparation of task, which students will undertake, is extremely important and, therefore, the e-moderator paid particular attention to the interests and needs of the group, whilst taking into consideration sociocultural factors. It was found that in establishing a momentum of successful constructivist learning, a spark was needed to stimulate and encourage students to contribute and engage with the chosen task or topic of discussion. As described by

Salmon (2002) a 'spark' is the stimulus or start provided to encourage interaction. One example of using a spark was when students were asked to complete the end of a sentence such as, 'I have always wanted to visit....', which then led to wider discussion around their chosen answers. Skinner (2009) asserts that if this spark is not provided, it can prove detrimental to the progression of the course.

The e-moderator's practice benefited from Jones and Peachey (2005) who demonstrated the importance of including a face-to-face element within the course, whilst also considering the implications of Salmon's model. Their study demonstrated that a face-to-face workshop prior to a course commencing was highly effective in assisting students with accessing the course, addressing technical issues and fostering subsequent socialisation. Regular face-to-face discussions with students were extremely important. This was achieved by the e-moderator arranging sessions with students via Skype and also enabling synchronous group discussions in Second Life. These proved to be pivotal in encouraging socialisation and interaction between students. White (2003) also influenced practice by indicating the strength of added synchronous assistance through introducing telephone tutorials into a course. This extra assistance offered advice and support whilst, at the same time, negotiating student needs and monitoring their progress throughout. The e-moderator consistently welcomed the implementation of synchronous one-to-one support sessions as they provided the opportunity to reassure, motivate and engage with students, encouraging them to complete tasks and at the same time enabling the e-moderator to address any persistent difficulties.

Utilising a journal as the chosen method for data collection proved to be effective in understanding the introspective thoughts of the e-moderator. However, after rigorously analysing the reflective journal, it was recognised that the e-moderator perhaps used it more as a personal diary to document feelings throughout the process. Although considerably insightful, they did not fully represent the richness of interactions or indeed consider the pedagogy employed during the process. It is therefore necessary for future practice to seriously consider the purpose of using a journal prior to conducting research using this particular method. Future research should include space to analyse more of the synchronous and asynchronous interactions demonstrated throughout the course with particular focus on feedback, motivation, reassurance and facilitation provided by the e-moderator. This would inevitably produce additional data to further explore the role of the e-moderator. In addition, and in accordance with Senior (2006), the e-moderator's journal should disclose the complexity of roles associated with e-moderation and demonstrate that facilitation is not the only role required. The e-moderator, therefore, also needs to constantly motivate and engage students and consistently monitor their progress throughout.

Utilising self-study methodology was effective for the purpose of this particular research. In focusing on the e-moderator it did, however, neglect the students' perspective. Future research will acknowledge this and a case study will be conducted which analyses the students' interactions, thus providing clearer indications and further proof of the stages detailed in Salmon's model. From an evaluation presented at the end of the course, it was evident that certain stages of the model were present giving an indication of its effectiveness. When asked about the technical support provided, one student stated, "the technical help was good. SL was a challenge, but the group meeting and exploring together helped a lot" (evaluation extract, see Appendix 9.1). This gives an indication of Stage One (Access and motivation) and Stage Two (Socialisation) of Salmon's model. The same student noted, "The most important thing I gained from this course is friendship" (evaluation extract, see Appendix 9.2) which indicated the importance of the socialisation stage. The constructivist approach and social cultural awareness were evident in the following feedback, "It was very interesting to see, that when we live in different countries and [have] a different upbringing, we have something in common. The love for music and nature, the dream to travel to other countries and learn about people at the other end of the world" (evaluation extract, see Appendix 9.3). Such feedback and evaluation of the course is beneficial for the e-moderator, provides material for reflection and delivers useful data for analysis, thereby providing additional results to enhance understanding of the effectiveness of the e-moderation process employed.

During the research process, the e-moderator was uncertain how much general intervention and encouragement should be provided in order to nurture interaction between students. Similarly, Moule (2007) reiterated this challenge in demonstrating the necessity of having such mediation for students to remain engaged but, at the same time, emphasised that a balance is needed, as too much interference can essentially stifle student interactions. She further stated that research results obtained were potentially weak, because of the small sample size used to conduct the research and emphasised that this factor, along with a limited amount of time, reduced the possibility of students forming a community of practice. These factors were present here and may have had an impact on the lack of opportunities for a variety of interactions. In acknowledging these factors, Murugaiah and Thang (2011) also indicated that it takes time to become acclimatised to such a learning environment. The e-moderator needs to understand these factors and to make efforts to consider sociocultural factors, whilst finding the most effective ways to reduce both their own initial anxieties and also those of the students through effective motivation and engagement. Therefore, in any future study, it would be beneficial to conduct more extended research to gain an understanding of what occurs over a much greater time period.

5.2. Conclusion

As identified in the Literature Review, more research should be conducted into the experiences of the e-moderator, highlighting the development and support required and the skills and responsibilities needed for successful e-moderation. This particular research attempted to address some of these needs and to provide the basis for subsequent research. It further explored the requirement needed to improve practice, along with providing insight and greater awareness of the e-moderation process, all with a view to supporting new e-moderators in their efforts to teach online. Although encountering a steep learning curve, the opportunity for the researcher to fully experience the e-moderation process has been an extremely informative and enlightening experience. Despite the problems and frustrations encountered en route, the positive aspects far outweigh the negatives and the researcher is very much aware that the benefits of the study are clearly worthwhile. Self-study research has proved to be highly rewarding, providing an awareness and understanding of the knowledge and requirements needed to undertake such a challenge. This has proved to be a constructive journey, in reflecting on and evaluating practice, which can prove to be beneficial to others in providing a valuable insight into this process.

This research has emphasised that teaching online not only requires facilitation and a sound knowledge of learning theories, but also an awareness of the complexity of other roles needed to become an effective e-moderator. Such roles were identified using Salmon's five-stage model and proved to be effective in scaffolding the process, although not necessarily preparing for the demands of successful e-moderation. These demands were fully realised through writing a reflective journal which was extremely beneficial in enabling the expression of frustrations and feelings throughout, whilst identifying the variety of problems encountered. Making this journal available online means that it can be accessed and used as an effective document, not only to identify what may happen in the process, but also to assist other practitioners who are similarly developing e-moderation skills and are new to, or about to start teaching online. From rigorously analysing the journal, it is strikingly evident how important it is to form an online Personal Learning Network to support and reassure the e-moderator and consequently reduce anxieties.

Before teaching online, it is essential to consider technological constraints and to carefully select appropriate Web 2.0 tools to complement constructivist learning. Furthermore, the e-moderator needs to be prepared to engage with and motivate students by providing well thought-out e-tivities (Salmon, 2002) and adopting a positive and encouraging attitude. Teaching language learners online has the added potential to break down cultural barriers and provide them with the confidence to interact effectively within a comfortable and supportive community. This can only be achieved by effective e-moderation and, therefore, teachers need to be fully aware of the skills involved to do this. Previous teaching experience is not sufficient to be able to teach effectively online and, certainly, this research suggests that undertaking some form of training, including specific experience of learning online, whilst exploring the affordances of technology is essential. This would give a greater understanding of, and an empathy with, what students will experience and also provide an awareness and competence with the e-moderation process. From the data analysed it was clear that Salmon's five-stage model was considerably effective for scaffolding e-moderation. However, it is evident that such a linear framework should not be used solely, and that other aspects must also be considered. It is suggested therefore, that the e-moderator acknowledges sociocultural factors and, in particular, the pedagogy employed to suit the specific course. This online journey leaves this new e-moderator with improved confidence, a greater awareness of previous research and a better theoretical understanding, as well as practical experience in working through the various challenges associated with teaching online. This process will, therefore, not only lead to better practice on a personal basis, but will also assist others who wish to embark on such an exciting and rewarding venture.

References

Adams, P. (2006). Exploring social constructivism: Theories and practicalities. *Education, 34*(3), 3-13.

Alaszewski, A. (2006). *Using diaries for social research.* London: Sage.

Aviv, R., Erlich, Z., Ravid, G., & Geva, A. (2003). Network analysis of knowledge construction in asynchronous learning networks. *Journal of Asynchronous Learning Networks, 7*(3), 1-20.

Ball, S., & Pearce, R. (2009). Inclusion benefits and barriers of "once-removed" participation. In Wankel, C., & Kingsley, J. [Ed.], *Higher education in virtual worlds: Teaching and learning in Second Life.* Bingley: Emerald Group Publishing.

Beetham, H., & Sharpe, R. (2007). *Rethinking pedagogy for a digital age: designing and delivering e-learning.* New York: Routledge.

Beldarrain, Y. (2006). Distance education trends: Integrating new technologies to foster student interaction and collaboration. *Distance Education, 27*(2), 139-153.

Bell, J. (2010). *Doing your research project* (5th ed.). Berkshire: Open University Press.

Benson, P. (2007). Autonomy in language teaching and learning. *Language Teaching, 41*(1), 21-40.

BERA. (2004). *Ethics and educational research,* [online]. Available from: http://www.bera.ac.uk/ethics-and-educational-research-2/, [Accessed 21 May 2011].

Berge, Z. L. (1995). The role of the online instructor/facilitator in facilitating computer conferencing: Recommendations from the field. *Educational Technology, 35*(1), 22-30.

Bruckman, A. (2002). *Ethical guidelines for research online,* [online]. Available from: http://www.cc.gatech.edu/~asb/ethics/, [Accessed 01 June 2011].

Campbell, C. (2009). Pedagogy, education and innovation in 3-D virtual worlds. *Journal of Virtual Worlds Research, 2*(1), 1-17.

Carr, N. (2010). *The shallows. How the internet is changing the way we read, think and remember.* London: Atlantic Books.

Clandinin, D. J., & Connelly, F. M. (2000). *Narrative inquiry: Experience and story in qualitative research.* San Francisco: Jossey-Bass.

Clandinin, D. J., & Connelly, F. M. (2004). Knowledge, narrative and self-study. In Loughran, J. J., Hamilton, M. L., LaBoskey, V. K., & Russell, T. (Eds.). *International handbook of self-study of teaching and teacher education practices.* Dordrecht: Kluwer.

Cochran-Smith, M., & Lytle, S. (1993). *Inside outside: Teacher research and knowledge.* New York: Teachers College Press.

Cohen, L., Manion, L., & Morrison, K. (2007). Research methods in education. London: Croom Helm.

Coia, L., & Taylor, M. (2009). Co/autoethnography: Exploring our teaching selves collaboratively. In Tidwell, D. L., Heston, M. L., & Fitzgerald, L. M. (Eds.). *Research methods for the self-study of practice.* Dordrecht: Springer.

Collinson, G., Elbaum, B., Haavind, S., & Tinker, R. (2000). *Facilitating online learning – Effective strategies for moderators.* Madison: Atwood Publishing.

Compton, L. K. L. (2009). Preparing language teachers to teach language online: A look at skills, roles, and responsibilities. *Computer Assisted Language Learning, 22*(1), 73-99.

Conceicao, S. C. O. (2007). *Teaching strategies in the online environment.* San Francisco: Jossey-Bass.

Davies, J. & Merchant, G. (2009). Negotiating the blogosphere: Educational possibilities. In Carrington, V., & Robinson, M. (Eds.), *Digital literacies: Social learning and classroom practices.* London: Sage.

Denzin, N. K., & Lincoln, Y. S. (2005). *The sage handbook of qualitative research* (3rd ed.). Thousand Oaks, CA: Sage.

Dey, I. (1993). *Qualitative data analysis: A user-friendly guide for social scientists.* London: Routledge.

Dudeney, G., & Hockley, N. (2007). *How to teach English with technology.* Pearson: Longman.

Dudeney, G., & Ramsay. H. (2009). Overcoming the entry barriers to Second Life in higher education. In Wankel, C., & Kingsley, J. (Eds.). *Higher education in virtual worlds: teaching and learning in Second Life.* Bingley: Emerald Group Publishing.

Feldman, A. (2003). Validity and quality in self-study. *Educational Researcher, 32*(3), 26–28.

Felix, U. (2002). The Web as a Vehicle for Constructivist Approaches in Language Teaching. *ReCALL, 14*(1), 2-15.

Garrison, R., & Anderson, T. (2003). *E-Learning in the 21st century: A framework for research and practice.* London: Routledge.

Goodfellow, R., & Lamy, M-N. (2009). *Learning cultures in online education.* London: Continuum Publishing.

Hample, R., & Stickler, U. (2005). *New Skills for new classrooms: Training tutors to teach languages and learning online* (3rd ed.). Cambridge: MIT Press.

Hockly, N. (2011). *The Principled Approach,* [online]. Available from: http://www.emoderationskills.com/?p=531, [Accessed 21 May 2011].

Hockly, N., & Clandfield, L. (2010). *Teaching online: Tools and techniques, options and opportunities.* Surrey: Delta Publishing.

IATEFL. (2011). *ELT Journal Debate 'Tweeting is for the birds, not for language learning', British Council,* [online]. Available from: http://iatefl.britishcouncil.org/2011/sessions/2011-04-17/elt-journal-debate-tweeting-birds-not-language-learning, [Accessed 21 May 2011].

Jauregi, K., Canto, S., Graaff, R., Koenraad, T., & Moonen, M. (2011). Verbal interaction in Second Life: Towards a pedagogic framework for task design. *Computer Assisted Language Learning, 24*(1), 77-101.

Jones, N., & Peachey, P. (2005). The Development of socialisation in an on-line learning environment. *Journal of Interactive Online Learning, 3*(3), 1-20.

Kitchen, J. (2009). Narrative self-study. In Tidwell, D. L., Heston, M. L., & Fitzgerald, L. M. (Eds.). *Research methods for the self-study of practice.* Dordrecht: Springer.

Koh, M. H., & Hill, J. R. (2009). Student perceptions of group work in an online course: Benefits and challenges. *Journal of Distance Education, 23*(2), 69-92.

LaBosky, V. K. (2004). The methodology of self-study and its theoretical underpinnings. In Loughran, J. J., Hamilton, M. L., LaBoskey, V. K., & Russell, T. (Eds.). *International handbook of self-study of teaching and teacher education practices.* Dordrecht: Kluwer.

Lankshear, C., & Knobel, M. (2006). *New literacies: Everyday practices & classroom learning.* Berkshire: Open University Press.

Lave, J., & Wenger, E. (1991). *Situated learning: legitimate peripheral participation.* Cambridge: Cambridge University Press.

Linconln, Y. S., & Guba, E. (1985). *Naturalistic Inquiry.* CA: Sage.

Lisewski, B., & Joyce, P. (2003). Examining the five-stage e-moderating model: designed and emergent practice in the learning technology profession. *ALT-J, 11*(1), 55-66.

Loughran, J. J. (2004). History and context of self-study of teaching. In Loughran, J. J., Hamilton, M. L., LaBoskey, V. K., & Russell, T. (Eds.). *International handbook of self-study of teaching and teacher education practices.* Dordrecht: Kluwer.

Loughran, J. J., & Russell, T. (2002). *Improving teacher education practices through self-study.* London: Routledge Falmer.

Mann, C., & Stewart, F. (2000). *Internet communication and qualitative research.* London. Sage.

Maor, D. (2003). The teacher's role in developing interaction and reflection in an online learning community. *Educational Media International, 40*(1), 127-138.

Marshall, C., & Rossman, G. (2006) *Designing qualitative research* (3rd ed.). Thousand

Miles, M., & Huberman, A. M. (1984). *Qualitative data analysis: A sourcebook for new methods.* CA: Sage.

Mishler, E. G. (1990). Validation in inquiry-guided research: The role of exemplars in narrative studies. *Harvard Educational Review, 60* (4), 415-42.

Mitchell, C., Weber, S., & O'Reilly-Scanlon, K. (2005). *Just who do we think we are? : Methodologies for autobiography and self-study in teaching.* New York: Routledge Falmer.

Mompean, A. R. (2010). The development of meaningful interactions on a blog used for the learning of English as a foreign language. *ReCALL, 22*(3), 376-395.

Monteith, M., & Smith, J. (2001). Learning in a virtual campus: The pedagogical implications of students' experiences. *Innovations in Education and Teaching International, 82*(2), 119-127.

Moule, P. (2007). Challenging the five-stage model for e-learning: A new approach. *ALT-J, Research in Learning Technology, 15*(1), 37-50.

Murray, L., & Hourigan, T. (2008). Blogs for specific purposes: Expressivist or socio-cognitivist approach? *ReCALL, 20* (1), 82–97.

Murugaiah, P., & Thang, S. M. (2010). Development of interactive and reflective learning among Malaysian online distant learners: An ESL instructor's experience.

International Review of Research in Open and Distance Learning, 11(3), 21-41.

Ng, K-C. (2001). Using e-mail to foster collaboration in distance education. *Open Learning, 16*(2), 191-200.

O'Dowd, R. (2007). *Online intercultural exchange: A practical introduction for foreign language teachers.* Clevedon: Multilingual Matters.

O'Dowd, R. (2009). Entering the world of online foreign language education: Challenging and developing teacher identities. In Goodfellow, R., & Lamy, M-N. (Eds.). *Learning Cultures in Online Education.* London: Continuum. Oaks, CA: Sage.

Oliveira, I., Tinoca, L., & Pereira, A. (2011). Online group work patterns: How to promote a successful collaboration. *Computers & Education, 57*(1), 1348-1357.

Oliver, M., & Shaw, G. P. (2003). Asynchronous discussion in support of medical education, *Journal of Asynchronous Learning Networks, 7*(1), 56-67.

Oncu, S. & Cakir, H. (2011). Research in online learning environments: Priorities and methodologies. *Computers & Education, 57*(1), 1098-1108.

Pachler, N., & Daly, C. (2011). *Key issues in e-Learning.* London: Continuum Publishing.

Pegrum, M. (2009). *From blogs to bombs: The future of digital technologies in education.* Crawley: UWA Publishing.

Pinnegar, S. E., & Hamilton, M. L. (2009). *Self-study of practice as a genre of qualitative research: theory, methodology, and practice.* London: Springer.

Pring, R. (2004). *Philosophy of educational research* (2nd ed.). London: Continuum.

Pritchard, A. (2007). *Effective teaching with internet technologies: Pedagogy and practice.* London: Chapman.

Rager, K. (2005). Self-care and the qualitative researcher: When collecting data can break your heart. *Educational Researcher, 34*(4), 23–27.

Richards, J. C., & Rodgers, T. S. (2001). *Approaches and methods in language teaching.* Cambridge: Cambridge University Press.

Rogers, J. (2000). Communities of Practice: A framework for fostering coherence in virtual learning communities. *Educational Technology and Society, 3*(3), 1-12.

Rovai, A. (2002). Building sense of community at a distance. *International Review of Research in Open and Distance Learning, 3*(1), 1-16.

Ryan, G., & Bernard, H. (2005). Data management and analysis methods. In Denzin, N. K., & Lincoln, Y. S. (Eds.). *The sage handbook of qualitative research* (3rd ed.). Thousand Oaks, CA: Sage.

Rymaszewski, M. (2008). *Second life: The official guide* (2nd ed.). Indianapolis: Wiley.

Salmon, G. (2002). *E-tivities: The key to active online learning.* London: Kogan.

Salmon, G. (2004). *E-Moderating: The key to teaching and learning online* (2nd ed.). London: Routledge.

Salmon, G. (2007). The Tipping Point. *ALT-J: Research in Learning Technology, 15*(2), 171-172.

Salmon, G. (2011). *E-Moderating: The key to teaching and learning Online* (3rd ed.). London: Routledge.

Scott, D., & Morrison, M. (2006). *Key ideas in educational research.* London: Continuum.

Senior, R. (2010). Connectivity: A framework for understanding effective language teaching in face-to-face and online learning communities. *RELC Journal, 41*(2), 137-147.

Siemens, G. (2004). *Connectivism: A learning theory for the digital age,* [online]. Available from: http://www.elearnspace.org/Articles/connectivism.htm, [Accessed 15 June 2011].

Skinner, E. (2009). Using community development theory to improve student engagement in online discussion: A case study. *ALT-J, 17*(2), 89-100.

Thomas, G. (2009). *How to do your research project.* London: Sage.

Thornbury, S (2011). *T is for Technology,* [online]. Available from: http://scottthornbury.wordpress.com/2011/05/01/t-is-for-technology/, [Accessed 21 May 2011].

Thurlow, C., Lengel, L., & Tomic, A. (2004). *Computer mediated communication. Social interaction and the internet.* London: Sage.

Tidwell, D. (2002). A balancing act: Self-study in valuing the individual student. In Loughran, J. J., & Russell, T. (Eds.). *Improving teacher education practices through self-study.* London: Routledge Falmer.

Vlachopoulos, P., & Cowan, J. (2010). Choices of approaches in e-moderation: Conclusions from a grounded theory study. *Active Learning in Higher Education, 11*(3), 213-224.

Vygotsky, L. (1978). *Mind in Society.* Cambridge: Harvard University Press.

Warschauer, M., & Kern, R. (2000). *Network-based language teaching: Concepts and practice.* Cambridge: Cambridge University Press.

Wenger, E. (1998). *Communities of Practice.* Cambridge: Cambridge University Press.

Wenger, E. (2009). *Digital habitats: Stewarding technology for communities.* Portland: CPsquare.

White, C. (2003). *Language learning in distance education.* Cambridge: Cambridge University Press.

Willis, D., & Willis, J. (2007). *Doing task-based teaching: A practical guide to task-based teaching for ELT training courses and practising teachers.* Oxford: Oxford University Press.

Appendices

1. Online course

Global Imaginarium:
http://globalimaginarium1.wordpress.com/

2. *Reflective journal*

Reflective Imaginarium:
http://reflectiveimaginarium.wordpress.com/

See Appendix 10 for full transcript.

Reflective Imaginarium
Journey of an e-moderator

Home About

Which Research Method?
May 19, 2011

I visited my tutor this week to discuss my thoughts and voice any concerns with the research proposal. Thankfully she was pleased with my new research poster and thought that my research would be very insightful and a worthwhile process. Please look at my Research Proposal Poster for a short summary of what I intend to do. My research will be 'An introspective account and critical evaluation of an e-moderators experience teaching in an online pilot EFL course.' I plan to collect data from this blog which will provide an introspective analysis throughout the process. I will outline Salmon's(2004) five stage model and see how it translates into practice. From the data analysis I will critically evaluate the model in relation to my practice and then seek to propose changes to the model.

85

3. Salmon's five-stage model

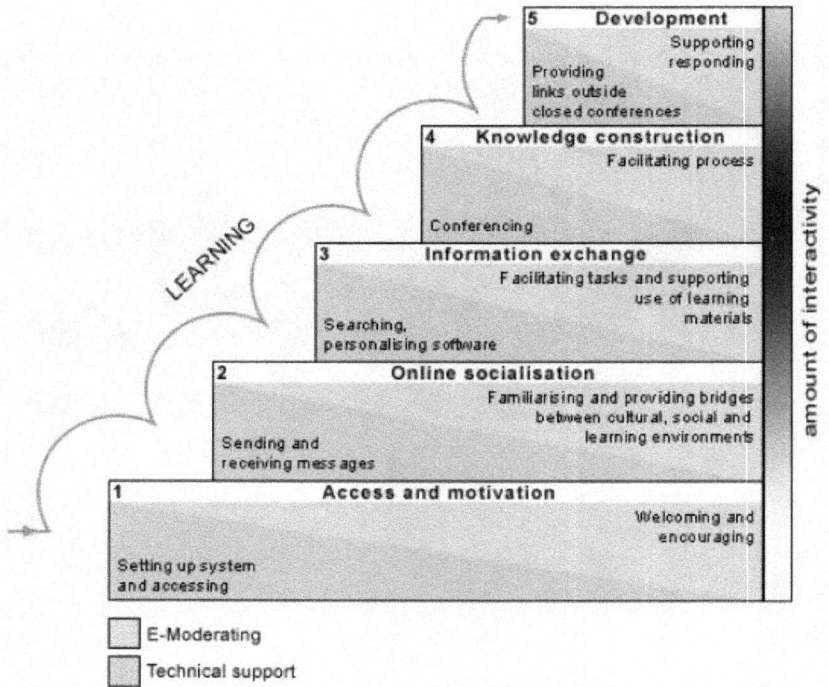

Salmon, G. (2004: 26). *E-Moderating: The Key to Teaching and Learning Online* (2nd ed.). London: Routledge.

4. Salmon's five-stage model adapted for Second Life

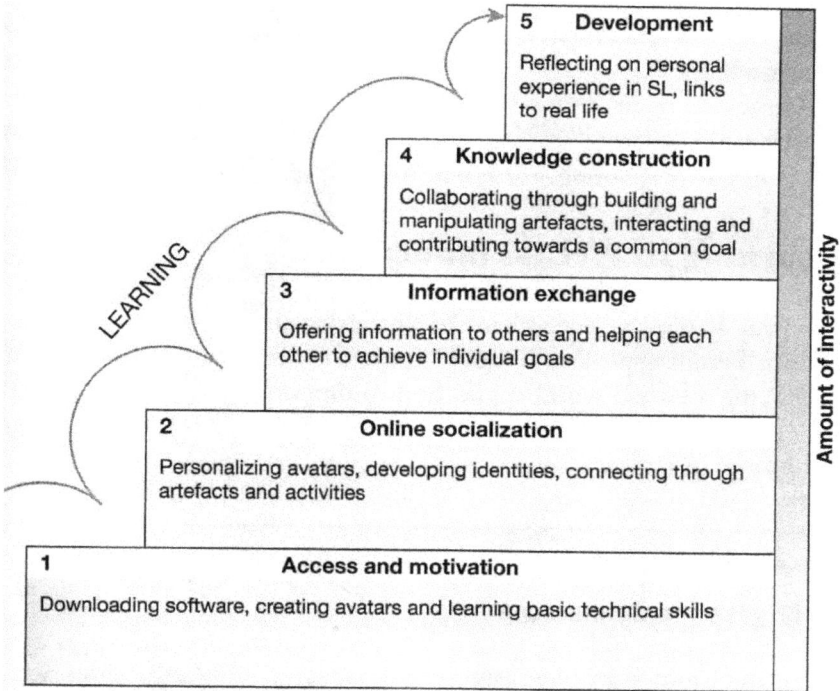

5   Development

Reflecting on personal experience in SL, links to real life

4   Knowledge construction

Collaborating through building and manipulating artefacts, interacting and contributing towards a common goal

3   Information exchange

Offering information to others and helping each other to achieve individual goals

2   Online socialization

Personalizing avatars, developing identities, connecting through artefacts and activities

1   Access and motivation

Downloading software, creating avatars and learning basic technical skills

LEARNING

Amount of interactivity

Model of teaching and learning in 3D virtual worlds

Salmon, G. (2011: 81). E-Moderating: The key to teaching and learning online (3rd ed.). London: Routledge.

5. The e-learning ladder

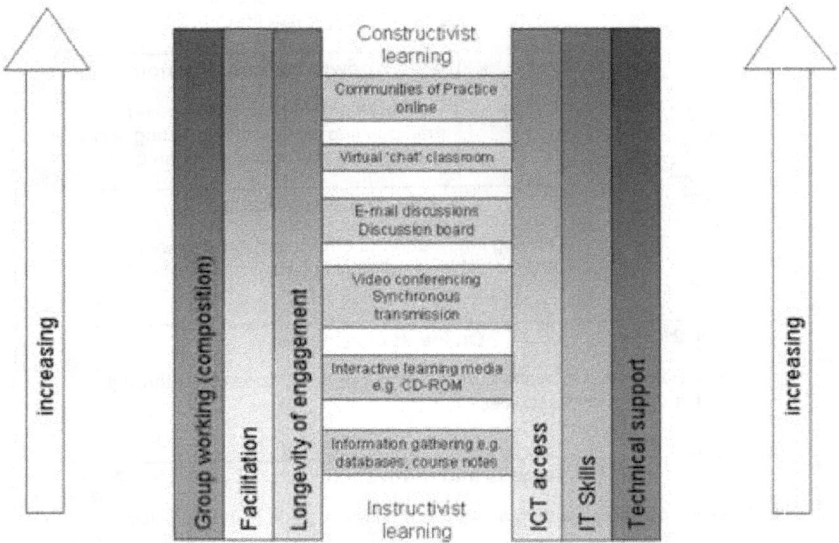

Moule, P. (2007: 41). Challenging the five-stage model for e-learning: A new approach. ALT-J, Research in Learning Technology, 15(1): 37-50.

6. The skills pyramid

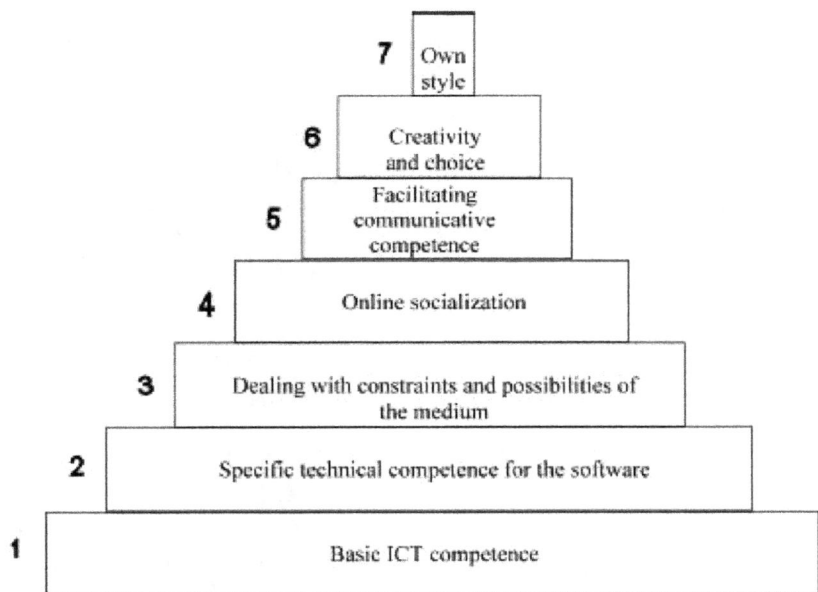

Hample, R., & Stickler, U. (2005: 317). New skills for new classrooms: Training tutors to teach languages and learning online (3rd ed.). Cambridge: MIT Press.

7. Online language teaching skills

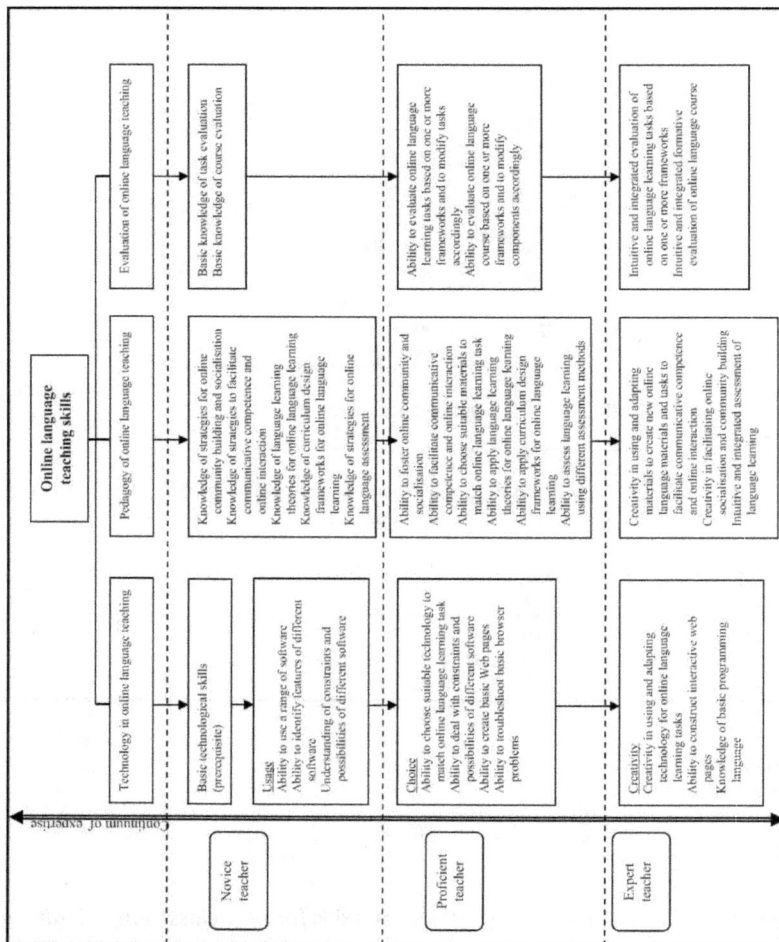

Compton, L. K. L. (2009: 82) *Preparing language teachers to teach language online: A look at skills, roles, and responsibilities. Computer Assisted Language Learning, 22(1): 73-99.*

8. Journal extracts taken from the e-moderator's blog, 'Reflective Imaginarium'

http://reflectiveimaginarium.wordpress.com/

8.1. *Finding participants (How difficult can it be?)* May 13, 2011
I reckon my first problem was believing that my snapshot of a course was innovative. When you finish creating a new course you feel very proud of what you have achieved and tend to not be as critical as you perhaps should. The more I step away from the course, the more I see changes that need to be made. However, I view it as a template which can be adjusted depending on my students' needs.

8.2. *The search continues (try not to panic).* May 14, 2011
It's astonishing how Twitter is such a powerful tool to create a buzz and connection with other practitioners. It really makes you feel that there are people interested and the sense of community encourages me to continue.

8.3. *Making Changes.* May 25, 2011
This is all very new to me and I suppose I was naive in thinking that I could incorporate so many tools into a short course. Furthermore, I don't have any experience teaching online so this will be a challenge and I fear that it will become a very stressful experience. However, I'm sure it will be an immense learning opportunity and at the end of the process I will have a great insight into teaching online.

8.4. *Keep calm & carry on.* June 20, 2011
Although students are not interacting as much as I would like to see on their blogs, I think that the gathering in SL really injected some much-needed energy and provided a platform

for students to interact synchronously in a supportive environment. It is uncertain what will happen each week and I need to understand that certain things out of my control will occur and instead of becoming stressed I will have to remain calm and carry on.

8.5. *The finishing line becomes the starting line.* June 26, 2011
It's now time to reflect on the process and use this as a basis to improve future practice and redesign the course to offer future participants a more beneficial experience. This has been an insightful experience into the complex role of the e-moderator and I've truly benefited from this process.

8.6. *Searching for a spark.* June 11, 2011
I managed to talk to the other student over Skype and they stated that they were very enthusiastic and excited about the course but due to starting a new job they could not find the time to start the first task, but would try their best over the next week to start interacting with other students and dedicate more time to the course. I need to realise that students are very busy and will not be able to dedicate all their time to the course. I feel that I should encourage them and make sure I'm available for any advice or assistance but there is only so much I can do and if they are too busy, then I should understand and try not to impose the course on them.

8.7. *Trying to avoid burn out.* June 20, 2011
This week has been extremely frustrating and I feel that my initial enthusiasm has burned out. I need to pick myself up and continue with positivity. I find it difficult to write a blog post when I'm feeling lethargic and I don't feel that it can fully capture my feelings.

8.8. *Searching for a spark.* June 11, 2011
I encountered several technical problems this week which hindered the progression of the tasks and created unneeded frustration with students. One student was unable to publish her new blog entry and sent me several e-mails detailing her frustrations.

8.9. *Trying to avoid burn out.* June 20, 2011
This is my first blog post this week as I have encountered problems with my internet connection which has meant that I have been unable to be fully available for corresponding with the students. It could not have happened at a worse time and I'm really hoping that the connection will be fixed in time for the SL meeting. I was concerned that my students' internet connections would be weak but never expected that my own connection would interfere with the course. Conducting a course online relies on a consistently strong network connection and it is extremely frustrating when technological problems occur which are out of my hands.

8.10. *Searching for a spark.* June 11, 2011
I can imagine how frustrating it must be to spend a long time writing a post and then not be able to publish it. I hope that this will not demotivate her to publish more posts.

8.11. *Initial anxieties can be overcome.* June 7, 2011
One student in particular stated that they had already tried to communicate with others in SL but had a very unsettling experience. They only wanted to practice conversational English but were frequently harassed and unsettled by some very explicit propositions. I was naively unaware of this happening in SL and from this found out that there can be a

problem with griefers who can make the SL experience very uncomfortable. I reassured the student and advised her to be careful as some places should not be visited in SL. I will make sure that students are aware of this and point them in the direction of places where they can safely practice conversation.

8.12. *Trying to avoid burn out.* June 20, 2011

I'm unsure how much attention I should provide and whether this will create too much reliance. However, I do feel that due to the nature of teaching online and the lack of physical presence that it is extremely necessary to engage with students and install a humanistic element so that they realise that even though there is a cyber-barrier created there is still connection and support available.

8.13. *The finishing line becomes the starting line.* June 26, 2011

Unfortunately, one student was unable to access the course this week due to not having any internet connection and therefore couldn't attend the SL meeting. I can imagine he must have been really frustrated. Due to having similar problems myself last week, I can empathise with his feelings of detachment. In light of this, I sent him an encouraging and reassuring email, which I feel is important.

8.14. *Searching for a spark.* June 11, 2011

The task instructions should be clear and the purpose made explicit so that students can understand why they are carrying it out. Perhaps my instructions are unclear and the purpose of the task may be vague. These are things I need to think about and consider when planning my tasks.

8.15. *Learning to juggle.* June 4, 2011
At first I was encouraged to see that students were using the comments boxes to introduce themselves but they did not seem to be interacting with each other. I need to realise that it will take time for students to socialise and I can't expect it to just happen.

8.16. *Learning to juggle.* June 4, 2011
It was very effective to talk with students and I was able to gain an understanding of how they were feeling at this early stage. After talking to the students on Skype I noticed that they started to comment more on other student's blogs and they also made more blog posts. It seems that the Skype chat made the course feel more personable and engaging due to the face-to-face element. At the same time students could practice their speaking and listening skills and share personal anecdotes.

8.17. *Initial anxieties can be overcome.* June 7, 2011
I'm very fascinated by the buzz of interaction and the students are sharing their thoughts and interests as well as their frustrations. Some posts in particular have created a surge of responses with some very personal and heartfelt communication. I'm delighted that students are engaging with each other and I didn't imagine it would be so productive in the first week.

8.18. *Trying to avoid burn out.* June 20, 2011
I felt that the course was starting to crumble around my feet and I searched inside for an answer to why this was happening. I thought that my course was not working and that the reason students were stopping the course was

because it was too time-consuming or unsuitable to their needs. I need to realise that it is uncertain what will happen during the course and I can't make myself fully responsible for students dropping out.

8.19. *Keep calm & carry on.* June 20, 2011

I decided use a more learner-centred approach where the students could practice their English and use it to share their own experiences and knowledge to interact with other students in a way that was personal and meaningful to them. I really felt that students were very involved in the discussion and I was inspired by their contributions. At the end of the session the students were extremely grateful for the experience and expressed enjoyment and positivity with the lesson. They thought that it was very relaxed and different to more conventional lessons.

8.20. *Keep calm & carry on.* June 20, 2011

Although students are not interacting as much as I would like to see on their blogs I think that the gathering in SL really injected some much-needed energy and provided a platform for students to interact synchronously in a supportive environment.

8.21. *The finishing line becomes the starting line.* June 26, 2011

After ten minutes of exploration I teleported them back to the classroom to discuss their experiences which they were very enthusiastic about. I believe that this session in SL was reflective and students took more control over the process.

9. *Evaluation extracts*

Taken from feedback provided on the course blog and an end-of-course survey conducted on *SurveyMonkey* (*https://www.surveymonkey.com/*).

Prior consent was provided by students to use their extracts for research purposes.

9.1. In response to the question: *Are you happy with the technical help you have received?*
28th *June 2011*:

"Yes, the technical help was good. SL was a challenge, but the group meeting and exploring together helped a lot."

9.2. *General comment on the course blog.* 28th June 2011:

"From the course I know how to use a tool like Second Life to learn English, to meet different people and to explore different places. I haven't written any blogs before, even a Chinese one. But now I enjoy writing blogs and sharing thoughts and feelings with you; I feel happy to see any comments on my blog as well as comments on your blogs. The most important thing I gained from this course is friendship."

9.3. *General comment on the course blog.* 27th June 2011:

"I learned about SL and how to deal with it. That was really something new. The blogs we had to write challenging and commenting on the others' blogs was good. I liked reading your posts and your opinions. It was interesting to hear you all speak your mind and find out about your countries and everyday life. Thanks for sharing your dreams and wishes for the future as well. It was very interesting to see, that even when we live in different countries and have a different upbringing, we have something in common. The love for music and nature for example, the dream to travel to other countries and learn about people at the other end of the world."

10. *Transcript of reflective journal*

Reflective Imaginarium
Journey of an e-moderator

<u>Which research method?</u>

May 19, 2011

I visited my tutor this week to discuss my thoughts and voice any concerns with the research proposal. Thankfully she was pleased with my new research poster and thought that my research would be very insightful and a worthwhile process. Please look at my <u>Research Proposal Poster</u>[1] for a short summary of what I intend to do. My research will be 'An introspective account and critical evaluation of an e-moderators experience teaching in an online pilot EFL course.' I plan to collect data from this blog which will provide an introspective analysis throughout the process. I will outline Salmon's (2004) five-stage model and see how it translates into practice. From the data analysis I will critically evaluate the model in relation to my practice and then seek to propose changes to the model.

Having decided on how to collect my data I was unsure what the research method was known as and whether it was considered valid research. Throughout my year learning about research methods I was well prepared to understand the differences between qualitative and quantitative research and made aware of the philosophical assumptions such as the ontological and epistemological stance of the researcher. Furthermore I learned about the different types of methods used to collect data towards adequately answering the particular research question. I thought that I was grasping the world of educational research until I started planning my own. My mind seems cluttered with so many

---

[1] See page 119.
Also available at http://reflectiveimaginarium.files.wordpress.com/2011/05/research-proposal-poster-new.ppt

different terms for methods and many of them seem to overlap and relate to one another. Whenever I read about the different methods I can relate most them to my research proposal. I thought it could be a case study in that I'm trying to conduct an in-depth analysis of my own perceptions. I also thought it could be action or practitioner research as I was following the process of my teaching practice and looking at how my practice influences the success of the course carried out. Or could it be Ethnographic or field study as I will submerge myself within the study. I was completely confused as my research intentions did not clearly fit into any of these methods. All I was certain of was that it would be a qualitative paradigm with an interpretivist stance. When I asked my tutor she cleared up my doubts and suggested that the methodology is known as self-study research and also critical research. During my year learning about research methods I was never made aware of these methods and I was a little anxious whether I would be comfortable carrying them out. My main concern was the subjectivity of the research and that I would not have a triangulation of data which would surely weaken my research. Again these doubts were reduced when my tutor stated that this type of research did not require a triangulation as it was just myself who was being researched and pointed me in the direction of some useful literature to assist with understanding the self-study method further. It's now time to go back to the books and hopefully gain a clearer understanding of the implications of the self-study method. This will assist with studying for my last assignment, which requires me to write a 2000 word research proposal and is due at the end of the month :(. The assignment will complete the Research Methods course providing a research proposal and indicates the start of the dissertation process. I now have a list of an unmanageable amount of literature to look through for particular references, which will hopefully be used to great effect in supporting my argument.

Making changes

May 25, 2011

At the moment I have been very busy finishing my last assignment before I can actually start the dissertation process. I have to say that I'm very anxious about what lies ahead. I really need to change the course which I developed as it has too many tools to cope with and I need to think of tasks which will be suitable for the learners needs. With not much time left to pursue my research I now need to restructure my course so that it is more manageable in the short time frame which I have. This is all very new to me and I suppose I was naive in thinking that I could incorporate so many tools into a short course. Furthermore, I don't have any experience teaching online so this will be a challenge and I fear that it will become a very stressful experience. However, I'm sure it will be an immense learning opportunity and at the end of the process I will have a great insight into teaching online.

I recently got in touch with Isil Boy who has a very helpful blog, offering many different ways to incorporate web 2.0 tools into practice and provides advice on how to use technology effectively to support language learning. Isil was very encouraging and offered me some advice which I need to seriously think about:

"I was just wondering about the number of the tools you used. Especially Second Life is a big challenge. Or, if you want to use more tools, creating a Mini Ning Network would be good to collect all the works on one place, and you can see all the members with their individual pages. Considering wikis, I use pbworks and embed "groupboard" for online chat and whiteboard, which is free ☺Maybe you can use it to make it available for synchronous communication. Finally, you can use #andy hashtag to chat with students."

This advice was a wakeup call and made me seriously consider whether I should make drastic changes to my course. I'm now starting to really question whether my course expects too much from the learners. Moreover, I don't want anxiety over the use of technology to distract them from the learning experience. I'm particularly nervous about teaching in Second Life as it is new to me and I'm taking a big risk including it in my course without much experience. I decided to contact Heike who is continually supportive and encouraging. She has agreed to meet me in Second Life to show me around and offer me advice and tips. I'm really grateful that Heike is willing to offer her time and I'm sure this will relieve some of my anxiety. I'm interested in discovering the benefits of language learning in Second Life and really don't want to erase it from my course as I think it is an exciting place for students to learn and offers a great potential for language learning.

Entering the unknown (strapped in and ready to go)

May 30, 2011

Today my course has officially gone live. The next four weeks I'm entering the unknown and I hope I enjoy the ride. As stated before this is my first time teaching online and my students are also new to learning in a fully online environment. At least I'm starting this journey with previous teaching experience and a copy of Salmon's e-moderation book as my trusty guide. I need to take a deep breath and embrace the unknown.

Since my last post I have been tied down with my last assignment which I just managed to submit today (phew!). Along with this I've chosen the participants and gave my course a well needed makeover. So it's been pretty full on and I'm expecting for it to get even busier as the month progresses. I need to start writing my literature review and at the same time give my 100% to the online course as well as keeping regular updates to this blog. I really want to try to make it as successful an experience as possible for the students taking part. The first stumble I encountered was technological difficulties. Thankfully I decided to make sure that prior to the course starting, students would check if they were able to download and access Second Life. Unfortunately two students were unable to do this due to having old computers with weak bandwidth. Luckily I made sure of this before starting. I don't want technology to interfere too much to the development of the course but I realise that it will create unavoidable problems which I need to address as they arise. I'm unsure how students will cope with creating their own blog and whether they will find difficulty when trying to add widgets along with adding videos and images to their blog posts. Hopefully I will be able to direct them via Skype if they are unsure how do to anything. Furthermore, I'm also extremely anxious about how students will react to using Second Life and I worry that I don't have enough experience using this platform to competently assist them through any difficulties they encounter. One student already voiced their concerns about using SL, asking if it was necessary to use it. I advised them to try not to worry about Second Life and told them that 'It is very new to me and my advice is just to go with the flow'. This is something I need to also repeat to myself. Even if I'm unsure and anxious I can't let students be aware of this and therefore, I need to remain as upbeat and confident as possible.

Learning to juggle (Stage 1 and 2)

June 4, 2011

Pheeeeeeeeeeeeeeeeeeeeeeeeeeeew! The course has gone live and I've reached the weekend with no disastrous stories to tell (touch wood). I hoped to find more chances to express my thoughts during the week but this is the only time where I've found I can sit back and reflect. Prior to the course starting I wanted to make sure that the students chosen for the course were able to access second life and had enough time during the week to dedicate to the course tasks. Students were chosen from different cultures so that there would be a more global atmosphere where students would have the opportunity to interact with others who they would otherwise not have had the opportunity to meet. The initial e-mails I received from students ranged from excitement to apprehension about what the course would entail. I really want make sure that everyone has a worthwhile experience.

The prior induction and first task incorporate the first (Access and motivation) and second stage (Socialisation) of Salmon's model. Students are greeted with a welcoming page and clear instructions are provided about how to take part with encouragement provided for students to engage with one another and interact. I was dubious whether I had provided enough information or even too much and wanted to get the right balance so that students were well-informed but at the same time not overwhelmed. Before releasing the first task I provided students with the course outline and netiquette and asked for them to introduce themselves. The first task requires students to write a blog post introducing themselves to the other students. Students are encouraged to read each others blogs and make comments on any posts which they find interesting. I wanted the task to be manageable so that students could become familiar with collaborating and comfortable creating their own blog. Salmon's model seems to only mention a Computer mediated conference (or forum), however I wanted to make sure that students could produce something which was self-directed and at the same time encouraged them to visit other students' blogs rather than just sharing the same platform. At first I was encouraged to see that students were using the comments boxes to introduce themselves but they did not seem to be interacting with each other. I need to realise that it will take time for students to socialise and I can't expect it to just happen. Therefore, I need to try my best at this early stage to encourage students to engage so that they can form a rapport with each other which can motivate students to support each other throughout and feel that they are not alone. A problem I noticed with using a blog for the course meeting place was that students were unsure where to put their comments. I need to make it clearer that the comments should be posted at the bottom of the corresponding task. I also feel that maybe having lots of different student blogs to look at may prove to be time-consuming and I wonder if it would have been better just having one platform like Moodle which has everything in the one place.

I have decided to incorporate a face-to-face synchronous component each week via *Skype* so that students can ask any questions about the course and express their feelings. At first I was apprehensive about talking over *Skype* and I was unsure whether this would be effective and worthwhile. After talking to three students I became more reassured and encouraged about using it. The students were very enthusiastic and expressed excitement about learning online and talking with me over *Skype*. Sharing my screen with the students was helpful in showing and talking them through the course blog and reassured them what was expected for each task. At the end of the conversation I issued each student with an mp3 recording of our conversation for them to reflect on what was said. Talking over *Skype* gave students an opportunity to talk about their feeling with regards to interacting with other students and the usage of technology. All students seemed to be comfortable with making their own blog and requested to be corrected if they make any errors. It was very effective to talk with students and I was able to gain an understanding of how they were feeling at this early stage. After talking to the students on *Skype* I noticed that they started to comment more on other students' blogs and they also made more blog posts. It seems that the *Skype* chat made the course feel more personable and engaging due to the face-2-face element. At the same time students could practice their speaking and listening skills and share personal anecdotes.

I have to say that I really enjoyed talking with the students but at the same time I'm completely exhausted. I have to make sure that I continue this blog as well as conduct the course and at the same time read relevant literature and start to write the dissertation. It's going to be a full on couple of months and I will just need to learn to juggle without dropping any vital components. Let's hope I become a competent juggler by the end of August.

Initial anxieties can be overcome

June 7, 2011

Task one has been a great success. The students have really made an effort to create their blog and have written some very insightful blog posts. The interaction has been enlightening with students commenting on each others post and writing very encouraging and supportive replies. I'm very fascinated by the buzz of interaction and the students are sharing their thoughts and interests as well as their frustrations. Some posts in particular have created a surge of responses with some very personal and heartfelt communication. I'm delighted that students are engaging with each other and I didn't imagine it would be so productive in the first week. The initial Skype chats proved to be very worthwhile with students expressing their excitement about the course and sharing any concerns they had so far. I used the time wisely to talk about any problems they were encountering with interaction and technology and emphasised that the course would work most effectively if everyone continually supported and interacted with each other.

It has not all been successful as two students have still not started the first task and I'm concerned with whether they will contribute to the course. I have tried to encourage them and sent e-mails reassuring that I can assist with any difficulties whether it be technological problems or anxieties related to interacting. I hope that they can still participate with the course but I'm unsure whether they will continue. I am aware that they may be following other students' interactions and may feel intimidated by sharing their own points of view and interests. This is known as *lurking* and although they appear to not to be participating they could still be showing an interest in the task without anyone knowing.

Students all stated that they were initially nervous about starting the course but felt more relaxed after talking over Skype and starting the first task. For several students this was their first time creating an online blog and although anxious at first they were able to successfully create one and start writing blog posts. Initially some students were unsure about publishing their writing online but realised the benefits and were excited about sharing their thoughts with others. I reassured students and explained that the most important thing about writing a blog post is the content and they don't need to worry as much about making mistakes.

Most of the students also expressed anxiety about using SL. Again I tried to reassure them that it takes time to get used to this new virtual environment and showed empathy by expressing that I'm also very new to SL and understand their anxiety. One student in particular stated that they had already tried to communicate with others in SL but had a very unsettling experience. They only wanted to practice conversational English but were frequently harassed and unsettled by some very explicit propositions. I was naively unaware of this happening in SL and from this found out that their can be a problem with *griefers* who can make the SL experience very uncomfortable. I reassured the student and advised her to be careful as some places should not be visited in SL. I will make sure that students are aware of this and point them in the direction of places where they can safely practice conversation.

All in all it's been a very encouraging and eventful experience. I'm excited to continue and look forward to seeing how task two develops. In accordance with Salmon's model it seems that students are ready to start stage three; Information Exchange, where students will find and exchange meaningful information with each other which should provide a spark to encourage interaction towards forming a community of practice.

Searching for a spark

June 11, 2011

I was encouraged by the first week's task and very excited for the students to start task two. However, It's been such contrast to the first week and I feel that the magic and buzz of the initial excitement has diminished and a strange quietness has emerged. I feel a little deflated by this and I'm hoping that things start to pick up otherwise I fear that the course is going to rapidly grow cobwebs and the tumbleweed is going to pass through my empty virtual town. Last week I mentioned that two students did not seem to be participating with the task or interacting with the other students. I sent some personal e-mails to them asking if everything was okay and if I could assist in anyway. One student was very apologetic and explained that due to personal reasons could not take part in the course. I managed to talk to the other student over Skype and they stated that they were very enthusiastic and excited about the course but due to starting a new job they could not find the time to start the first task but would try their best over the next week to start interacting with other students and dedicate more time to the course. I need to realise that students are very busy and will not be able to dedicate all their time to the course. I feel that I should encourage them and make sure I'm available for any advice or assistance but there is only so much I can do and if they are too busy then I should understand and try not to impose the course on them.

I encountered several technical problems this week which hindered the progression of the tasks and created unneeded frustration with students. One student was unable to publish her new blog entry and sent me several e-mails detailing her frustrations. I could tell from the messages that she was very frustrated and really wanted to publish her new post. She gave me her blog password to see if I could assist with publishing it. I was concerned that she gave me her password but it meant that I could see what was wrong and make sure that her post was published. I can imagine how frustrating it must be to spend a long time writing a post and then not be able to publish it. I hope that this will not demotivate her to publish more posts. When talking with her on Skype she shared her screen with me and I was able to advise her how to publish the post and we eventually sorted out the problem. Talking on Skype has proved successful as the students are able to voice their concerns and also their excitement with the course. There are however frequent problems with the clarity of sound and it can prove to be frustrating when the voice cracks up and the reception slow down. Along with this any background noises can be an interference and adds to the frustration. Students expressed that they understood the task but did not feel it was easy to locate an English blog to share with other students. Also the link I provided on my blog did not work and Chinese students were unable to view the YouTube videos which I posted. I wondered if the task was not meaningful for them and suggested that they share a website/blog which they follow even if it is not in English and then share their thoughts about it with the rest of the group. I thought that students would enjoy discovering new English blogs/websites but maybe this is not the case and they do not see the purpose for carrying out this task. According to Salmon stage three, *information exchange* should provide an activity which requires students to share information which they have gathered. It is important for students to think about how this information can benefit themselves and others. The task instructions should be clear and the purpose made explicit so that students can understand why they are carrying it out. Perhaps my instructions are unclear and the purpose of the task may be vague. These are things I need to think about and consider when planning my tasks.

I planned to meet students in second life so that they could become familiar with the basic functions and it would provide an induction before meeting with the other students. I encountered several problems in SL. Firstly I teleported the student to where I was and then I explained the basic function such as flying and sitting down. I then explained how to text chat and use the voice chat. For some students their voice chat was very distorted and it became very frustrating for both of us so we had to resort to typing messages. Another student's voice was good however they expressed that they would prefer to talk on Skype as it was clearer. It took a long time to explain the basic functions in SL and I have to say it was difficult to explain how to do things without seeing their screen. The time scheduled to meet in SL was also problematic as the time in China appeared to be a peak time for people using the internet which made it very difficult for students to log on. Although there were several unavoidable problems the students did express excitement about using SL and realised how it benefits for networking. One student told me that they really liked using SL and in particular liked shopping and talking in English with people from other countries. I was very encouraged by this.

I realise that this post has been longer that I initially expected but I feel that I need to document these frustrations. I find it difficult to write regular posts due to a busy schedule during the week and I can completely understand how students must feel about writing regular posts. I need to make sure I can encourage students to continue with the tasks but at the same time I need to understand that there needs to be a spark so that students feel it is worthwhile to engage. Learning online means that students can easily hide and if they see that other students are not contributing then they may feel less encouraged. It needs to continue to be positive and try my best to motivate and engage students through encouraging e-mails and making myself available. I also need to lower my expectations and evaluate the tasks provided.

I recently talked to Heike Philps on second life about using second life as a component for my online course. We talked about the logistics of attempting to schedule a group meeting with students from different continents. It is not easy to make sure that students can meet together at a convenient time when their time zones are very different. She suggested that students maybe overwhelmed at first by such a new environment and instead of creating complex tasks it is preferable to lower my initial expectations and instead try to create a relaxed atmosphere by just sitting down and chatting. Heike is very encouraging and her calm and relaxed persona on SL makes it comfortable to interact.

Trying to avoid burnout

June 20, 2011

This week has been extremely frustrating and I feel that my initial enthusiasm has burned out. I need to pick myself up and continue with positivity. I find it difficult to write a blog post when I'm feeling lethargic and I don't feel that it can fully capture my feelings. As stated in my previous post there was an uncomfortable absence of communication around the course recently and students did not appear to be contributing to the task. I decided to send a motivating email to students asking if I could assist them in any way and informed them that they should not hesitate to contact me with regards to any problems or queries they were having. From this email I received replies from two students who were unable to continue with the course. They were extremely apologetic and explained that due to personal circumstances, could no longer participate. I felt that the course was starting to crumble around my feet and I searched inside for an answer to why this was happening. I thought that my course was not working and that the reason students were stopping the course was because it was too time-consuming or unsuitable to their needs. I need to realise that it is uncertain what will happen during the course and I can't make myself fully responsible for students dropping out. On a more positive note the remaining students were starting to contribute to the task which included finding a blog/website of interest to them and luckily interaction was flowing again. However, most students made me aware that they were very busy and could not dedicate as much time to the task as they had initially intended. I was also made aware that they were finding it difficult to find a blog/website which interested them enough to share with others which contributed to them being unable to complete the task earlier. I need to realise that students may find certain task more difficult to complete than others and rather than imposing my own ideas it is important to create tasks which are flexible.

A further concern is that interactions may become lessened between the students because there are only four left. Also, my initial proposal of creating a multicultural community is not taking shape and perhaps I set my sights too high. It is difficult to install autonomy in students and perhaps I should have made sure that each student had a personal plan/time schedule to follow during the week where they would make sure at designated times to contribute to the course. Maybe students are dedicating more time to the course than I think, however it is really difficult to gauge how much time they are actually spending. My main priority is to encourage students by providing continual positive reinforcement and make them aware that I am available. I'm unsure how much attention I should provide and whether this will create too much reliance. However, I do feel that due to the nature of teaching online and the lack of physical presence that it is extremely necessary to engage with students and install a humanistic element so that they realise that even though there is a cyber-barrier created there is still connection and support available.

I decided to meet students in Second Life instead of Skype this week for a 1-2-1 session because I have organised a group meeting in SL this Saturday so I wanted to make sure that initial SL anxieties could be alleviated and offer them a brief orientation to prepare them for communicating with others through voice and text chat. This was the perfect opportunity to find out how comfortable they were using Second Life and to assist with practicing the basic functions. Students were very receptive and appeared to really enjoy and learn from the experience. They all expressed that they were really looking forward to meeting the other students in SL.

This is my first blog post this week as I have encountered problems with my internet connection which has meant that I have been unable to be fully available for corresponding with the students. It could not have happened at a worse time and I'm really hoping that the connection will be fixed in time for the SL meeting. I was concerned that my students internet connections would be weak but never expected that my own connection would interfere with the course. Conducting a course online relies on a consistently strong network connection and it is extremely frustrating when technological problems occur which are out of my hands. I'm half way through and I need to make sure that both the internet and my mind are healthy and strong enough to continue positively with this process and avoid burn out.

Keep calm & carry on

June 20, 2011

This week could have ended in a disaster but after a successful lesson in Second Life I started to feel that things were not as bad as I thought. My dependence on the internet really hit home last week. I suffered with no connection for a week due to 'technical difficulties in the area'. Every time I phoned my supplier they advised that the problem would be sorted very shortly but very shortly turned into what seemed like an eternity and I slowly felt that the online course was falling on its face. I thought that it would just be a small glitch but when it was still not working by Friday I started to really panic as the SL meeting had been planned for Saturday morning. Fortunately my family helped out and they were able to find me a quiet place with internet connection (and some strong coffee) in order to conduct the lesson. I realise that I can't fully depend on my internet connection and always need to consider what to do if the connection fails. Luckily during this time I was able to use the free internet in the University library however, if I was not at Uni it could have been very costly using internet cafes and I don't really want to intrude on anyone to borrow their internet. I managed to inform my students that I was having trouble with my home connection just in case they needed prompt responses to questions. Thankfully the students did not require any quick advice during this time. I suppose this inconvenience really made me consider how much I rely on the internet as I felt like I was coming down from a technological dependence and realised how much I was addicted to social networking online, never mind my whole Master's degree depending on it too.

Before meeting the students in second life I spent time planning a lesson and put a poster on the course blog to advertise the session and to provide students with some information of what was required for the lesson. The poster as well as the one-on-one induction session made sure that the students were fully prepared for the meeting in SL and I believe that this was necessary to make sure that the meeting would run as smoothly as possible. I have to say, I was a little nervous as to how the session would work but this was short-lived, because when the lesson started everything seemed to flow really well. I came prepared with discussion questions and made sure that there was a warm up and cool down activity. I feel that the students made the lesson such a success as they were really enthusiastic and comfortable in sharing their points of view and expressing themselves. The questions and topics chosen provided the needed spark to engage students in meaningful conversation. Each student was willing to provide their own opinion which added to the other students' contribution, whereby a range of views were provided resulting in construction of knowledge together. I did not really teach and instead I became a facilitator and manager of the discussion. I decided to use a more learner-centred approach where the students could practice their English and use it to share their own experiences and knowledge to interact with other students in a way that was personal and meaningful to them. I really felt that students were very involved in the discussion and I was inspired by their contributions. At the end of the session the students were extremely grateful for the experience and expressed enjoyment and positivity with the lesson. They thought that it was very relaxed and different to more conventional lessons.

Students produced some great blog posts this week and it seems that they are becoming more comfortable writing the posts and have started to add images and provide hyperlinks. This is really encouraging. At the same time, however, interaction between the students and the initial excitement to meet each other has reduced. Although students are not interacting as much as I would like to see on their blogs I think that the gathering in SL really injected some much-needed energy and provided a platform for students to interact synchronously in a supportive environment. It is uncertain what will happen each week and I need to understand that certain things are out of my control will occur and instead of becoming stressed I will have to remain calm and carry on.

The finishing line becomes the starting line

June 26, 2011

The task this week required students to explore SL further and write a blog post about their experiences. One student was frustrated with her experience because she could not find the place she was searching for.

On the other hand, another student really enjoyed visiting some places and even created a slide show of his exploration, however like the other student he couldn't find anyone who wanted to engage in conversation. Encouragingly one student had fully embraced second life and expressed that she felt very comfortable interacting with others. During conversation she referred to a few residents as her best friends in SL, with whom she meets on a regular basis on a variety of sims.

This task encouraged students to be reflective and critical of their experience which was evident in their blog posts. Unfortunately one student was unable to access the course this week due to not having any internet connection and therefore couldn't attend the SL meeting. I can imagine he must have been really frustrated. Due to having similar problems myself last week, I can empathise with his feelings of detachment. In light of this, I sent him an encouraging and reassuring email, which I feel is important.

This weeks meeting in SL again showed that the strengths of using this virtual platform for educational purposes greatly outweigh the weaknesses. Initially there were problems with students logging on and with the voice chat slowing down or breaking up throughout. Apart from these disturbances, the session was really worthwhile and the students appeared to be enjoying the experience. I also felt more relaxed in this environment and tried to strengthen my facilitation skills through listening carefully to what students were saying, asking them to expand on statements, encouraging everyone to share their views and making sure that I chose certain topics to develop conversation.

The conversation flowed nicely, but I needed to be aware of the time in order to cover the topics planned, but at the same time encourage interactions which students were engaged with. Within the conversation, students frequently reflected on their experiences in SL. I drew on a student who was becoming more familiar with SL to advise students on the best way to interact with other residents in SL. This really benefited the others as they were apprehensive about interacting in SL. The advice this student offered was encouraging. I suggested that the same student take the others on a quick trip to a place of her choice. The idea was to exploit the immersive environments potentials for conversation. After ten minutes of exploration I teleported them back to the classroom to discuss their experiences which they were very enthusiastic about. I believe that this session in SL was reflective and students took more control over the process.

At the end of our session I asked students to offer their opinions about the course. All students mentioned that expressing their feelings and interacting in English through their blogs and in group meetings in SL had increased their confidence in such away that they felt more encouraged to take their IELTs test so they could study in other countries. Positivity was expressed for both blog writing and using SL and they explained that they would continue to use these platforms in the future. I was especially pleased to hear this, as one of my main objectives was to improve their confidence expressing themselves in English and also to introduce different WEB 2.0 tools which could encourage autonomous and constructivist learning.

The month has not been as successful as I would have liked it to be, but I believe that the students have benefited overall from taking part in the online course. I made sure that the requirements to complete each task were clearly outlined and provided examples of what was expected. Although, while this can be highly time-consuming I firmly believe it made the process more understandable for the students and reduced any problems occurring during the week.

My course has come to an end and its now time to reflect on the process and use this as a basis to improve future practice and redesign the course to offer future participants a more beneficial experience. This has been an insightful experience into the complex role of the e-moderator and I've truly benefited from this process. The course has now finished but it's just the start for both myself and the students to continue learning within such a stimulating and evolving environment with endless opportunities.

The end is just the beginning

June 26, 2011

So, here it is, my finished reflective journal, documenting my one month journey as an e-moderator on a self-created online course. I hope my journey can provide other practitioners with an insight into the process of e-moderating for the first time. I now need to analyse the data captured in this journal and include this analysis in my dissertation. Here's hoping I manage to complete it on time and successfully pass (fingers crossed). I would be delighted if this journal can benefit other researchers, practitioners or MSc students. I also hope it will provide a document for others to reflect on and critique.

An introspective account and critical evaluation of an e-moderators experience teaching in an online pilot EFL course.

Andy Webster (s1013230)— MScTESOL Edinburgh University

Abstract

This dissertation will explore the processes involved with teaching an online efl course. It will consider how effective Salmon's five stage model can assist in preparing a new e-moderator to successfully teach in an online environment. Qualitative research will be carried out which will involve an analysis of the e-moderators reflective journal. In depth data will be collected which will evaluate my approach to on-line teaching and critically appraise the skills needed to become a successful e-moderator.

Rationale

"Teaching online is not the future anymore. It is an important part of the here and now of language teaching education. Teachers need to know what tools are out there and what techniques can help them use these tools." (Clandfield, 2010: 3)

It is no longer necessary for learning to be confined to the classroom. The online environment provides flexible learning, where students can contact with learners globally and learn at their own pace. This dissertation will assist in evaluating my first experience of teaching online and will explore how my development relates to Salmon's Five stage model. My perceptions and attitudes towards teaching in a fully online environment will be analyzed thoroughly

Research Design and Methods

The following questions will be addressed in accordance with teaching in an on-line environment.

• How can computer mediated communication be used effectively to encourage learning on-line ?
• Can face-to-face language learning pedagogy translate to an on-line learning environment?
• Does Salmon's five stage model adequately prepare an e-moderator for the complexity of an on-line language learning environment?
• What is the teachers role in an on-line learning environment?
• What challenges does an e-moderator face when teaching on-line for the first time?
• What are the e-moderators beliefs and perceptions about teaching within an on-line language learning environment?

The e-moderator will keep a reflective journal prior to and during a one month on-line course. This will then be analysed thoroughly and the role of e-moderator in accordance with Salmon's Five Stage model will be critically evaluated. This will provide a greater understanding of the processes and challenges encountered when teaching online for the first time

Timetable For the Dissertation

Date	Section	Activity
May	• Literature Review • Methodology	• Write up literature review • Write up method and design
June	• Field Work	• Conduct field work • collect data
July	• Analysis • Discussion	• Analyse data and write findings • Write discussion
August	• Conclusion • Finish	• Write Conclusion • Proof read

Communicating via the Web 2.0 tools

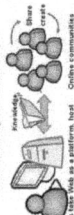

Users take Web as a platform, host | Online communities

"Teachers' must learn to recognise the social processes that technology enables and understand how to support these processes as a way to foster the emergence of meaningful communities." Wenger(2009:191)

Literature in the Area of Study

• Beetham, H and Sharpe, R.(2007) Rethinking pedagogy for a digital age: designing and delivering e-learning. New York: Routledge
• Compton, L. K. L. (2009) Preparing Language Teachers to Teach Language Online: A Look at Skills, Roles, and Responsibilities. Computer Assisted Language Learning, 22(1): 73-99.
• Goodfellow, R. & Lamy, M-N. (2009) Learning Cultures in Online Education. London: Continuum Publishing
• Hockley, N and Clandfield, L. (2010) Teaching Online Tools and Techniques, Options and Opportunities. Surrey: Delta Publishing
• Murugaiah, P. & Thang, S. M. (2010) Development of Interactive and Reflective Learning Among Malaysian Online Distant Learners: An ESL Instructor's Experience. International Review of Research in Open and Distance Learning, 11(3): 21-41.
• Pachler, N and Daly, C. (2011) Key Issues in E-Learning. London: Continuum Publishing
• Salmon, G. (2002) E-tivities: the Key to Active Online Learning. London: Kogan
• Sensor, R. (2010) Connectivity: A Framework for Understanding Effective Language Teaching in Face-to-Face and Online Learning Communities. RELC Journal, 41(2): 137-147.
• Wenger, E. (2009) Digital Habitats: Stewarding Technology for Communities.Portland: Cpsquare.

Point of departure: the original research proposal poster (See p.99).

EFL Communication Strategies in Second Life
An exploratory study

by Susan Gowans

The Second Life sessions referred to in this book were also the subject of a research paper by Susan Gowans. The edited version of this paper is available from LinguaBooks under the title *EFL Communication Strategies in Second Life: An exploratory study*.

The analysis of the session transcript reveals the extent to which the participants employed many of the communication strategies concomitant with face-to-face interactions for effective conversation management. The data also shows that the participants adapted their communication strategies to suit the Second Life platform, thus overcoming conversational ambiguities arising from the absence of paralinguistic signals.

Discourse analysis of the transcript offers further insight into power relations, politeness and risk-taking strategies and provides signs of sociocultural learning and language development in keeping with Second Language Acquisition theory.

www.ingramcontent.com/pod-product-compliance
Lightning Source LLC
Chambersburg PA
CBHW071839090426
42737CB00012B/2303